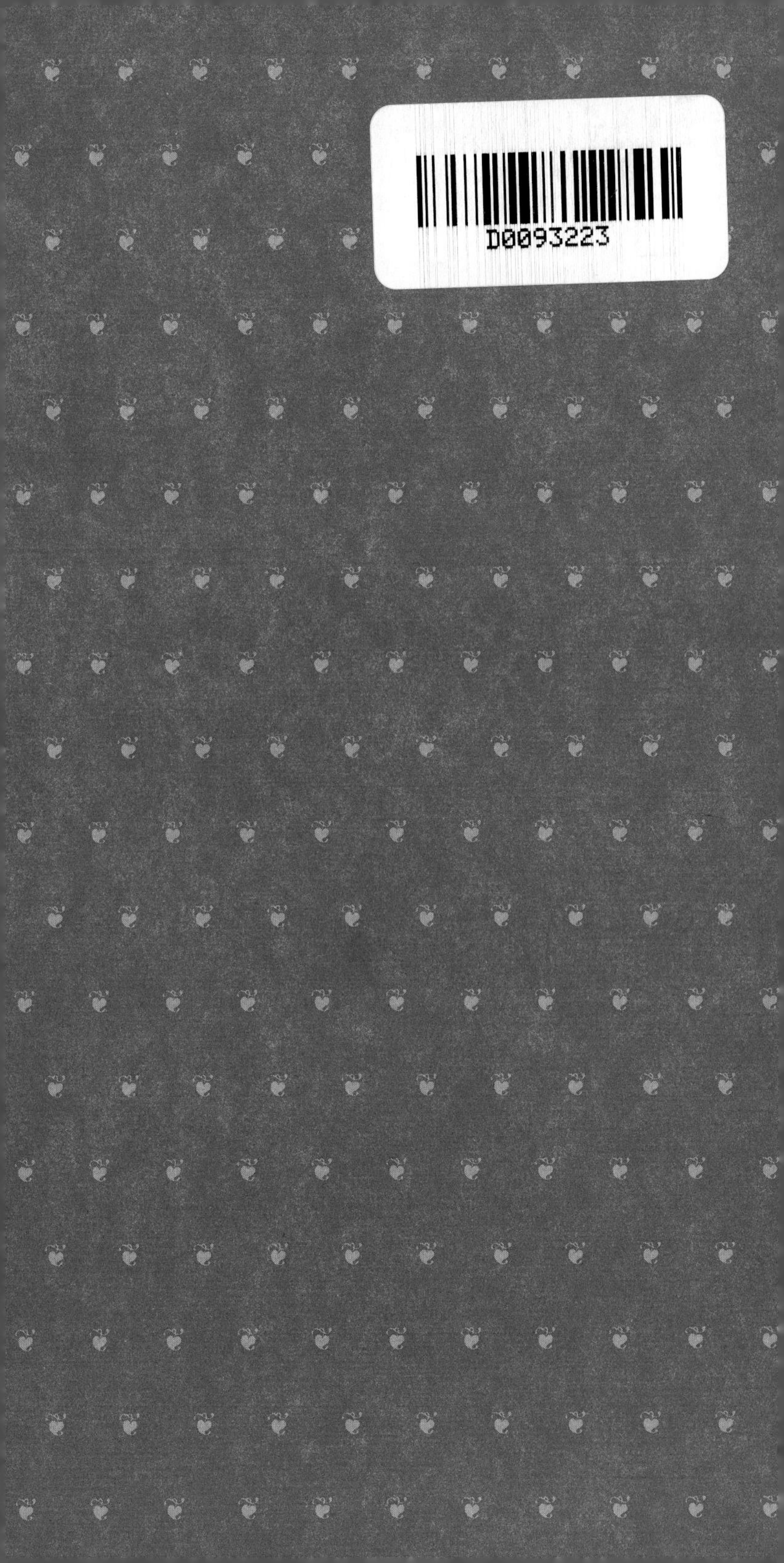

PRUNING

DAVID SQUIRE

PRUNING

DAVID SQUIRE

Illustrated by Vana Haggerty

TIGER BOOKS INTERNATIONAL
LONDON

Designed and conceived by

THE BRIDGEWATER BOOK COMPANY LTD

Art Directed by PETER BRIDGEWATER

Designed by TERRY JEAVONS

Illustrated by VANA HAGGERTY FLS

Edited by MARGOT RICHARDSON

CLB 3373

This edition published in 1994 by

TIGER BOOKS INTERNATIONAL PLC, London

Printed and bound in Singapore

ISBN 1-85501-384-3

CONTENTS

SHAPING THE ENVIRONMENT

MAN has never been satisfied to leave the shapes of plants solely to the efforts of Mother Nature. Pruning and shaping them has, therefore, been an important part of his gardening activities.

Some historians consider that civilization strode alongside the spread and development of grapevines. Whether or not this is accurate, it is true that there was a vast range of early pruning equipment for shaping plants.

The Romans developed many pruning tools while spreading the cultivation of grapes. One of these tools, a *falx vinitoria*, had a hooked blade with sharp cutting edges on both sides. This was secured to a strong handle about 30cm/12in long. A variation on the *falx vinitoria* was the *falx arboraria*, which had a curved blade with a cutting edge on the hooked side and resembled the modern billhook. It was primarily used to prune vines and sever stems too thick for a knife. Machetes and pangas, used as tools and weapons of war, are variations of these and still available throughout the world.

As well as slashing and cutting tools, there were early saws.

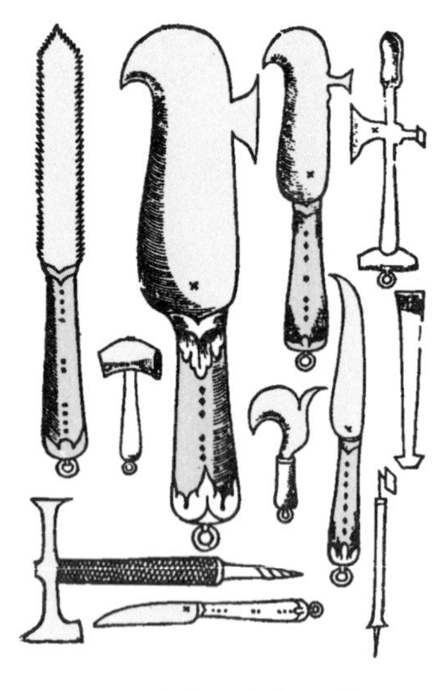

EARLY *gardening tools for pruning and grafting were functional if not sophisticated by modern standards. Here, from a sixteenth-century book, is revealed a wide range of implements. Several of these are the ancestors of today's knives, saws and axes. By the late nineteenth century tools were becoming refined, with sharper cutting edges and folding handles for knives and saws.*

EARLY *engravings, like this one from the sixteenth century, often show gardeners pruning and training plants.*

YEWS AND CHURCHYARDS

Yews have for many centuries been planted in churchyards. These handsome, evergreen shrubs and trees were often grown in ancient times near places of worship and death. Indeed, in the language of flowers, yew symbolizes sorrow.

With the advent of Christianity, yews, like so many features of earlier religions, were freely embraced. Another suggestion about yews being in churchyards – and thereby protected – is that they provided a source of wood for the construction of longbows.

THRASHING TREES!

Pruning is not solely reserved for cutting off stems and shoots: the crude practice of either stripping off leaves or subjecting a shrub or tree to a 'sound thrashing' has also been practised.

In tropical and subtropical areas, unfruitful mango trees were beaten with a long, pliable bamboo cane. Although seldom recommended now, it successfully retarded exuberant growth and thereby encouraged the development of fruit. This thrashing encouraged an adaption of the old and unflattering adage:

A wife, a dog, and a mango tree,
The more you beat them the better they be.

PRUNING WITH SMOKE

If any technique used to encourage fruiting is a form of pruning, then voluminous smoke produced by burning wood and rubbish is another one. In some countries, damp wood was ignited under barren fruit trees to encourage the development of fruit.

Bark ringing and root-pruning are other techniques to encourage fruitfulness but they are infrequently used nowadays. The introduction of less robust root-stocks with predictable vigour has made these techniques unnecessary. However, in warm countries vigorous fig trees, which continually develop leafy growth at the expense of fruit, are frequently brought into fruitfulness by root-pruning. Mango trees were also frequently root-pruned.

INTERLACING PLANTS

Pleaching dates back several centuries and involves forming hedges on stilts. Romantic arbours were also partly formed in this way. Lime trees, Hornbeam and beech are frequently used, but wisteria and ornamental vines offer attractive alternatives, especially in narrow, confined areas. Plant young trees 2.4–3m/8–10ft apart, in two rows with about 3.6–4.5m/12–15ft between them, depending on the area and perspective. Once the trees have grown 3-3.6m/10-12ft high, cut off all lower branches and train the upper ones along strong wires. Prune the upper framework to shape in autumn or winter.

PHILOSOPHY OF PRUNING

FEW gardening skills are cloaked in as much mystique as pruning. It is performed mainly on woody plants, such as ornamental and fruiting trees, shrubs, hedges and roses, and mainly involves the removal of stems and branches. This directs a plant's activities in several ways, including shaping, regeneration of shoots, larger and more attractive flowers and regular production of fruits. It also keeps plants healthy and encourages a long life-span.

In warm climates, the objectives of pruning also include the development of straight, clean stems, essential in rubber cultivation; twisted or bent stems for use in furniture construction; and the development of wide-spreading trees that create shade. Additionally, nipping out growing tips from tea plants encourages an abundance of fresh, young shoots.

MANY *flowering shrubs are pruned each year to encourage the development of flowers. Forsythias flower in spring and are pruned as soon as their flowers fade. However,* Hibiscus syriacus, *flowering from mid-summer to early autumn, needs no more pruning than to cut off straggly shoots. The Common Broom* (Cytisus scoparius), *which bursts into colour during late spring and early summer, needs pruning after flowering.*

TIMING

The time of the year when plants are pruned is important. Basically, pruning is a task solely dictated by the type of growth a plant has and when it is dormant. Invariably, this inactive period is influenced by the weather and in particular by winter. In tropical and subtropical regions, droughts frequently enforce periods of dormancy, but for gardeners in temperate regions the dictating factor is cold weather.

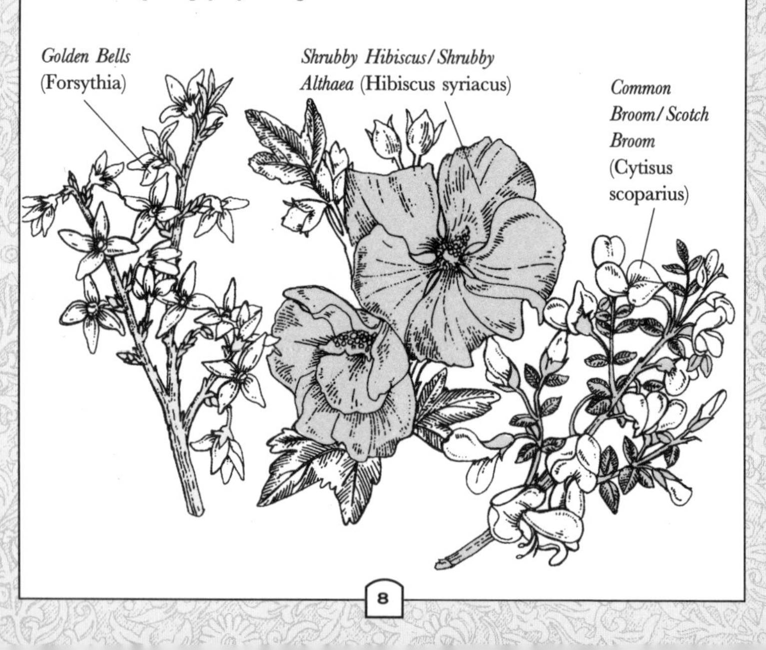

Woody plants, such as ornamental and fruiting trees, are invariably pruned during their dormant period. However, peaches, nectarines, apricots, cherries, plums and gages are susceptible to silver leaf disease and to reduce the risk of spores entering cut surfaces they are pruned in spring when growth is beginning. Conversely, trees with sappy wood, such as birches, Horse Chestnuts, conifers and some maples are likely to bleed profusely if cut during summer when their sap is flowing strongly. Therefore, prune them in late autumn or early winter.

BROKEN, *diseased and misplaced branches must be removed. Cut off branches, pare surfaces smooth and coat with fungicidal paint.*

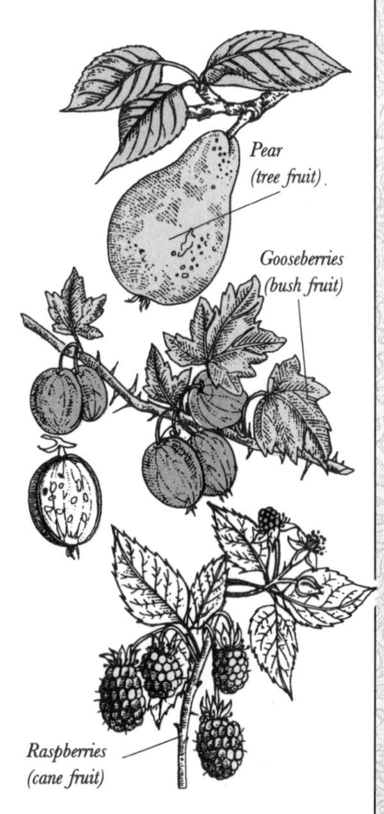

ALL *fruiting plants need yearly attention, whether growing as trees, bushes or canes. If this is neglected, yields decline and individual fruits are small and poor in quality. Pruning fruit trees, bushes and canes is detailed on* *pages 42–59.*

INFLUENCING FLOWERING

If cold winter weather was not an influencing factor, pruning could be performed immediately an ornamental shrub finished flowering, leaving the maximum amount of time for the development of fresh shoots before its blooming period during the following year. In warm regions this is possible, but where frosts and low temperatures are experienced, any pruning performed late in summer is likely to encourage soft shoots that would be damaged later.

For this reason, in temperate regions, deciduous flowering shrubs are divided into three main groups:

- Flowering in winter: prune immediately flowering ceases. Little pruning is usually needed.
- Developing flowers from spring to early and mid-summer: prune directly the flowers fade, so that ensuing growth has time to ripen before the onset of winter.
- Flowering in late summer: prune in early to mid-spring of the following year.

These are the general rules, but shrubs grown for their attractive stems, such as the dogwoods, are exceptions. These are severely pruned in mid-spring, cutting stems just above the ground.

EQUIPMENT YOU WILL NEED

THE range and quality of pruning and hedging tools has improved dramatically during recent years. High-quality steel gives knives and secateurs keen cutting edges, plastic handles reduce maintenance and introduce longevity, while power tools make gardening even more of a pleasurable pursuit.

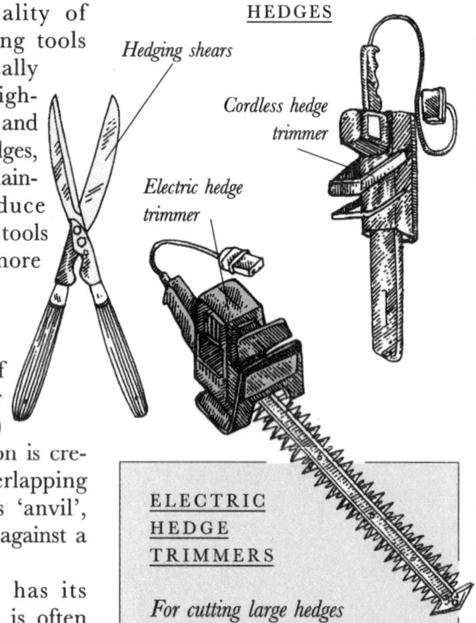

SECATEURS

There are two types of secateur: 'bypass' (earlier known as parrot models) is where the cutting action is created by one blade overlapping the other. The other is 'anvil', when a sharp blade cuts against a base known as an anvil.

Each of these types has its devotees; the anvil type is often preferred by professionals because replacement parts are available.

The bypass type has a more surgical cut than the anvil model, which, if the cutting blade is blunt, may bruise stems.

Both types are available in a range of sizes, most cutting 15mm/5/8in stems, while heavy-duty types cut up to 25mm/1in.

Most secateurs are sold to suit right-handed people, but left-handed types are available.

LOPPERS

These are like large secateurs and have similar cutting actions – bypass or anvil. Loppers with handles 38–45cm/15–18in long cut shoots up to 36mm/1 1/2in thick, but heavy-duty types, with handles 75cm/2 1/2ft long, sever 5cm/2in wood.

Some anvil types have a compound cutting action, enabling thick shoots to be easily cut.

HEDGES

Hedging shears

Cordless hedge trimmer

Electric hedge trimmer

ELECTRIC HEDGE TRIMMERS

For cutting large hedges without becoming unduly tired, an electrically-powered trimmer is essential. But ensure there is a power-breaker (also known as a circuit-breaker) fitted into the circuit so that if the cable is severed the power is immediately cut off.

CUTTING *blades range in length from 33–75cm/13–30in. A few have cutting knives on one side only; others cut on both, making them user-friendly for both left- and right-handed people. Some trimmers have dual reciprocating blades.*

STORING AND LOOKING AFTER TOOLS

The life expectancy of all garden tools depends on the way they are used and stored.

- *Don't force secateurs to cut branches too thick for them – the blades soon buckle.*
- *After use, wipe away all residue, especially sap.*
- *Wipe bright-metal parts with an oily rag.*
- *At the end of the pruning season, clean and wipe wooden handles. Smear with linseed oil.*
- *Most handles nowadays are plastic and only need to be occasionally wiped clean.*
- *Hang up tools in a damp-proof, airy shed or garage. Peg boards are ideal places.*
- *Regularly check cables for damage and have all electrical equipment inspected every year by a competent electrician.*
- *Keep sharp-edged tools out of reach of children.*

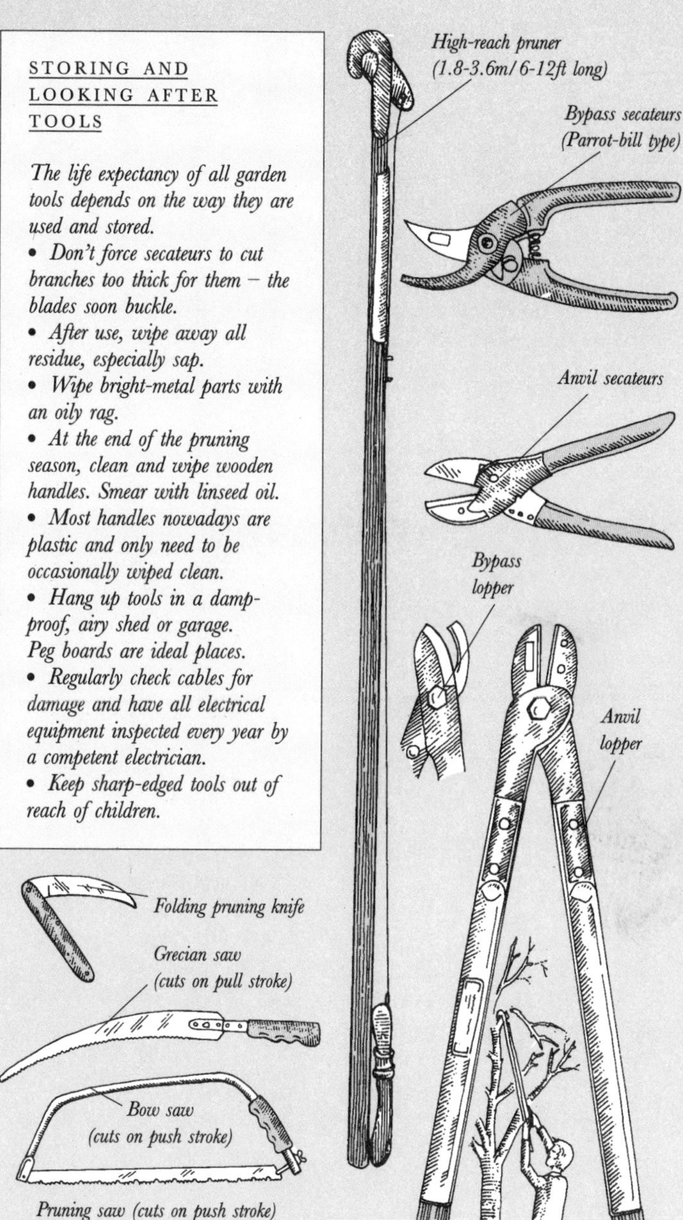

SAWS *are essential for cutting off large limbs. Easily-accessible branches are best cut with a bow saw, but in confined areas a Grecian type is easier to use.*

Using a high-reach pruner

PRUNING CUTS

SECATEURS, loppers, knives and saws are the best tools with which to remove shoots, stems and branches. However, in addition to the 'when and how' of pruning individual plants, it is essential that cuts are made in the right positions relative to buds and other shoots.

TOO HIGH OR TOO LOW

Each pruning cut must be slightly above a bud – not so high that a small stub of the shoot remains above it, nor so low that the cut leaves the bud perched high above it. A range of pruning cuts is shown at the bottom of this page.

As well as each cut being positioned slightly above a bud, to encourage a shrub or tree to develop outwards, the bud that remains must point in the desired direction. If buds point inwards they eventually create a congested central part of the plant. Air circulation is reduced and the presence of diseases encouraged.

WEEPING NATURE

On plants with a cascading nature, it is essential that cuts are made to leave buds on the upper sides of stems. This helps to create a better weeping appearance than if they are cut to leave downward-pointing buds.

THE ROSE FACTOR

In recent years, different ways to prune roses have been tested by the English magazine *Gardening Which?* in conjunction with the Royal National Rose Society. Three different methods of pruning roses are being tested:

- using secateurs in a careful and traditional manner
- using secateurs but in a rough way – not just above buds
- using a hedge trimmer.

The results have amazed many gardeners: floribundas (now called cluster-flowered roses) produced better-quality and more flowers when pruned roughly with secateurs or hedge trimmers than traditionally and carefully with secateurs. Hybrid teas (now known as large-flowered roses) were as good

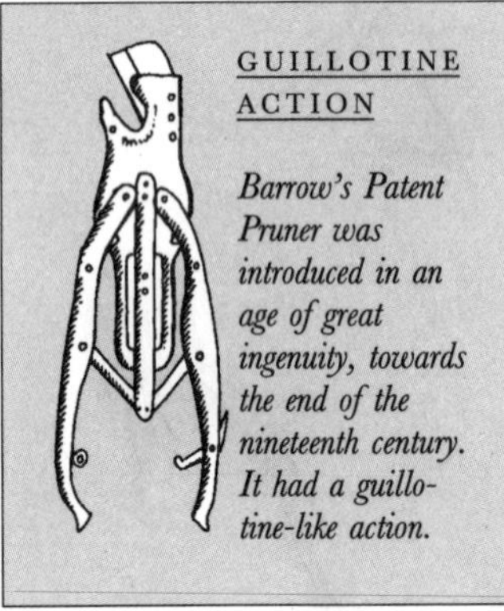

GUILLOTINE ACTION

Barrow's Patent Pruner was introduced in an age of great ingenuity, towards the end of the nineteenth century. It had a guillotine-like action.

PRUNING CUTS

All pruning cuts should be made at a slight angle and just above a bud. Only the cut on the right is correct: the others are too high or low.

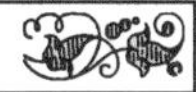

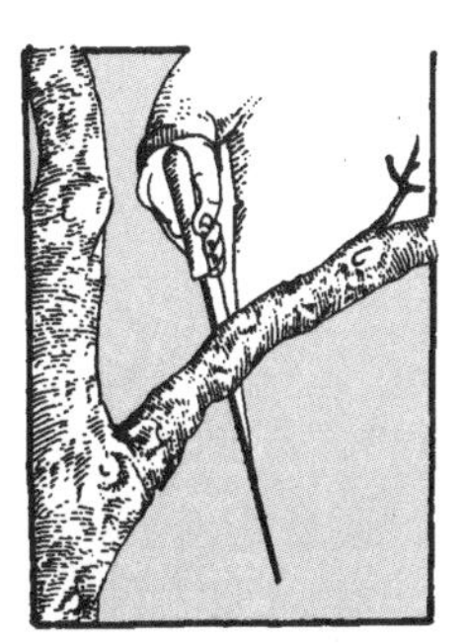

1. CUT *off a large branch by initially cutting it about 30cm/12in from the trunk. First, make a cut on the lower side, then complete the cut from above. Cut back apple and pear trees in winter when dormant.*

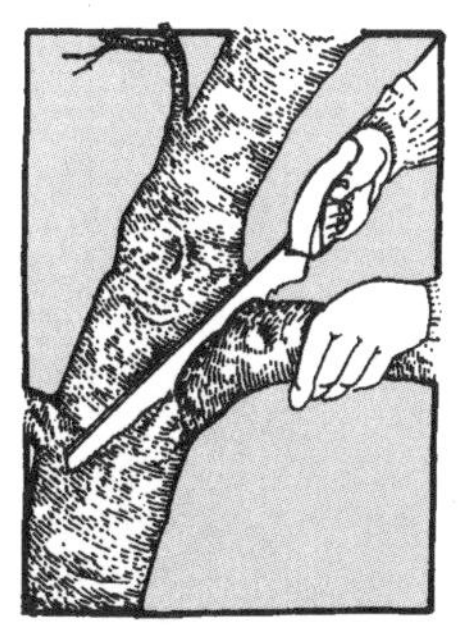

2. USE *a saw to cut off the short stub. Saw from above and hold the stub to prevent it falling and damaging the bark. Use a sharp saw – more accidents occur from blunt tools than sharp ones that cut wood easily.*

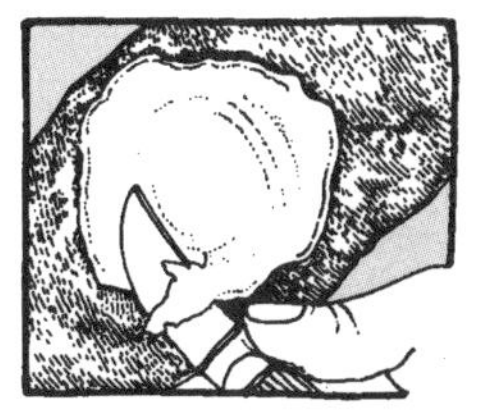

3. USE *a sharp knife to smooth the cut area, especially at its edges.*

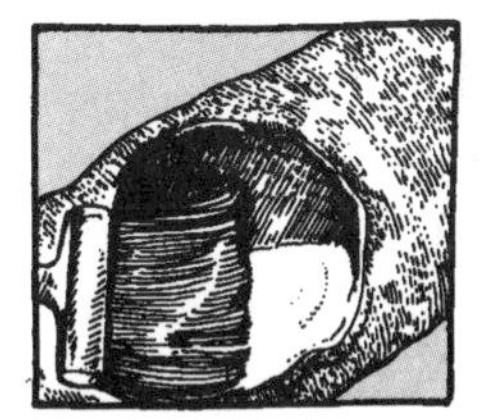

4. PAINT *the cut area with fungicidal paint to help it heal and to prevent the entry of diseases. Use an old brush for this job.*

with the rough technique and hedge trimmer as when carefully pruned with secateurs.

The long-term effects of pruning with hedge trimmers are yet to be known, as well as evaluating the wisdom of not cutting to outward-pointing buds.

POLLARDING

To most gardeners, pollarding is just another term for butchering trees! It is invariably performed on trees that have grown too large for the area in which they were originally planted.

It is a technique of cutting all branches back to the tree's crotch. This results in a mass of vigorous stems growing straight up from the trunk. Invariably, after several years, the tree has to be pollarded again often making it unsightly.

Sometimes, pollarding is necessary where roads have been widened or buildings constructed too close to the trees. However, the moral of this is to select trees with shapes and sizes that suit the areas in which they will grow.

LIFE, LIMBS AND EYES

Powered hedge trimmers as well as chain-saws have changed gardening out of all recognition during the last twenty years, but there is a price to be paid:

- *Don't use them during wet weather or on wet hedges.*
- *Ensure children and domestic pets are indoors.*
- *Always use a power-breaker.*
- *Wear goggles to prevent dust or splinters going in your eyes.*
- *If you are right-handed, move from left to right while using a hedge trimmer: vice versa for left-handed gardeners.*
- *Either use a cable harness, or loop the power lead over your shoulder to keep it safe.*
- *Wear stout gloves and a thick coat while using a chain-saw – do not wear a scarf or tie.*

PRUNING AND CLIPPING HEDGES

HEDGES have several functions in gardens: creating perimeters and forming internal barriers that provide shelter and privacy. Some are evergreen, others deciduous. A few develop flowers but most are grown for their foliage.

Once planted, hedges last for many years and if they are to remain attractive they must be pruned regularly and properly throughout their lives. Early pruning is essential.

Basically, there are three types of hedges: formal and deciduous, and coniferous.

FORMAL DECIDUOUS HEDGES

These must be pruned immediately they are planted. If left to grow naturally, their bases become bare of shoots and leaves. Directly after being planted, cut all shoots back by a half to two-thirds.

If bare-rooted plants have been used, this will be at any time from late autumn to early spring. Hedges formed from container-grown plants – which can be planted at any time whenever the soil is not frozen or waterlogged – are pruned immediately after they are planted.

As well as encouraging shoot-packed bases, shortening a plant's growth reduces the risk of strong winds rocking plants and loosening their roots in early years.

During the second year, again use secateurs to cut back all new shoots by half to two-thirds. Although continually cutting back hedges in this manner may appear drastic, if neglected the hedge will be ruined. Sometimes, pruned hedges initially look unsightly.

During the third year, use hedging shears or electric hedge trimmers to cut the new stems back by

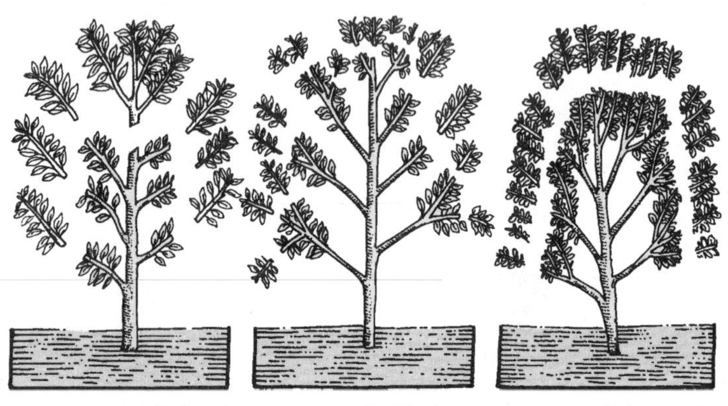

1. PRUNING *newly planted deciduous and formal hedges is essential. If plants are neglected at this stage, their bases become bare of shoots and look unsightly. Cut all shoots back by half to two-thirds to ensure bushiness.*

2. DURING *the following year, cut back all new shoots by half to two-thirds. Although cutting back plants in this manner may appear drastic, eventually it creates a fully-clothed hedge, from its top to the base.*

3. IN THE *third year, cut the new stems back by one-third and during subsequent years by about the same amount. Regular clipping – three or four times a year – is essential if the hedge is to remain attractive.*

SHAPING *a hedge so that it has a uniform outline is easily achieved by forming a wooden template. It is an ideal guide when cutting back hedges that have become neglected.*

one-third. In subsequent years, regular clipping is essential – at least three or four times a year.

KNOT GARDENS

An early description of knot gardens comes from Venice in about 1499, where the background to knot-like figures was filled with herbs and flowers. Nearly a century later, the English gardener Thomas Hill in *The Gardener's Labyrinth* mentions knot gardens set in thyme and hyssop.

In Tudor times, from about 1485 to 1605, knot gardens were usually rectangular beds with intricate patterns outlined in Edging Box, Rosemary or even Thrift.

INFORMAL HEDGES

Like formal hedges, these too must be cut back after planting to encourage the development of bushy shoots from ground level. This is especially important, as many informal hedges are grown for their flowers and if initial pruning is neglected the base will be bare of flowers.

Neglected flowering hedges are easily identified by their bare bases and flowers borne high up.

During subsequent years, leave informal hedges to develop naturally. However, if the hedge is not making much side growth, cut back the top shoots in spring by removing half of the growth made during the previous year.

Many informal hedges have large leaves, so therefore only use secateurs or long-handled loppers. If hedging shears are used, they chop up leaves and create an unsightly hedge.

Always cut just above a leaf-joint, and the best time is in spring or autumn, when excessive growth is most apparent.

Cutting back old, neglected hedges that are full of dust is a dirty job. As well as wearing old clothing, take care to use protective goggles to prevent dust getting into eyes, and also to prevent shoots poking in eyes.

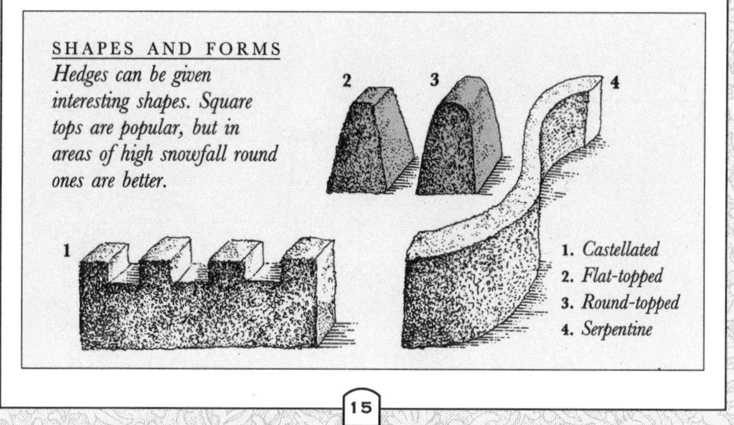

SHAPES AND FORMS
Hedges can be given interesting shapes. Square tops are popular, but in areas of high snowfall round ones are better.

CONIFEROUS HEDGES

ALTHOUGH not all conifers are evergreen, those used to create hedges are. They include many attractive forms of *Chamaecyparis lawsoniana, Thuja plicata* and *Thuja occidentalis,* as well as the exceedingly fast-growing *x Cupressocyparis leylandii.*

Coniferous hedges should not be pruned when planted. They naturally develop shoots from their bases, although long shoots can be trimmed back in spring.

DESIRED HEIGHT

When the hedge reaches the desired height, cut 15–30cm/ 6–12in off the leading shoots. During the following year, the hedge will thicken and hedging shears or electric hedge trimmers should be used to trim the sides.

When planting conifers – or any other boundary plant – remember that with age a hedge thickens dramatically.

RENOVATING OLD HEDGES

Eventually, hedges become too large, usually because of excessive vigour or neglect.

- If the hedge is too wide and high, correct this over two or three years. In early spring of the first year, use long-handled lopping shears to cut back top growth. The following year, cut back one or both of the sides.
- Not all hedging plants can be severely cut back, but those that can include: aucuba, beech, Box, elaeagnus, forsythia, Gorse, hawthorns, Hornbeam, Privet, pyracantha, rhododendrons, Sweet Bay and yew.
- Large, straggly hedges of Rosemary and lavenders are best pulled out and replaced.
- Conifers, with the exception of yew, should not be cut hard back. Instead, pull out and replace them. However, the tops of conifers can be cut out, but the result is not always attractive.

WHEN *the leading shoots on conifers rise 15–30cm/ 6–12in above the desired height, cut them off. Stretch a garden line between the hedge's ends to ensure it is cut at a uniform height. Use secateurs or loppers.*

WHEN *pruning large-leaved evergreen hedges, use secateurs (left) rather than hedging shears that shred large leaves and make them unsightly. Cut out dead shoots (right) close to the bases of hedges. Also, pull away and remove all dead leaves.*

CREATING ROMANTIC ARBOURS

LEAFY arbours packed with scented plants and climbers usually evoke thoughts of a romantic and perhaps mystical age long passed. Indeed, William Shakespeare, at the end of the sixteenth century, wrote:

Love-thoughts lie rich when canopied with bowers.

A bower, by the way, is a shaded, leafy recess, although it is possible that Shakespeare partly used its poetic meaning – a private chamber or boudoir.

TRAINING *plants to create unusual features has been a continual pursuit of Man. Here is a seventeenth-century engraving of an arbour where friends could be entertained.*

CONSTRUCTING AN ARBOUR

These need not be large or expensive: a few brick or wooden columns and a roof create an attractive framework. They can be soon covered by climbers such as wisteria or Mountain Clematis. The pruning of these is described on pages 20 and 21; roses are other candidates and their pruning is detailed on pages 40 and 41.

LEAFY *bowers, packed with scented flowers and colourful leaves, create secluded, restful and contemplative places in which to relax*

SCENTED CLIMBERS FOR ARBOURS

- Japanese Wisteria *(Wisteria floribunda)*. Pendulous, violet-blue, vanilla-scented flowers.
- Mountain Clematis *(Clematis montana)*. Pure-white, sweetly-scented flowers.
- Fragrant Virgin's Bower *(Clematis flammula)*. Small, white, hawthorn-scented flowers.
- Common White Jasmine *(Jasminum officinale)*. White and jasmine scented.
- Orange-peel Clematis *(Clematis orientalis)*. Yellow, bell-shaped, nodding, slightly sweet flowers.
- Honeysuckle *(Lonicera japonica)*. White to pale yellow, sweetly-scented flowers.

TOPIARY

CLIPPING and shaping plants dates back to the Romans and Pliny the Elder, in the first century AD. It became so popular then that even the name of the topiarist was often depicted in clipped Box.

After the decline of the Roman Empire, topiary also ceased, although in the Middle Ages plants were trained and clipped, often upon frames formed of thin, flexible stems, such as osier (Willow).

RENAISSANCE REVIVAL

A revival took place in Renaissance Italy in the second half of the fifteenth century, with plants formed into geometric shapes, human figures and animals.

The gardens at Hampton Court Palace in England were also decorated at the end of the sixteenth century with topiary, which gained such popularity that even Rosemary was trained and clipped.

In about 1629, the gardener and herbalist John Parkinson recommend Privet for topiary, adding that Thrift, lavenders, Germander and thyme were also widely used.

THE FRENCH CONNECTION

During the seventeenth century, the fashionable French-inspired parterre gardens were created: plants performed the role of embroidery against a background of coloured earth or bands of turf. This gave fresh impetus to topiary and evergreen plants such as yew, holly, laurel and Bay that were widely used to create pyramids, balls and other figures.

Large-leaved evergreens became especially fashionable and desirable because large topiary figures could be created from them.

UNFASHIONABLE

During the latter part of the eighteenth century, the passion for topiary declined and it was considered to be old-fashioned. But in the early part of the following century it was partly revived during the construction of gardens that wished to recapture the atmosphere of earlier years.

Although gardening on the grand scale ceased to use topiary, it nevertheless survived in cottage gardens, frequently depicting animals.

Yew, Box and the Shrubby Honeysuckle *(Lonicera nitida)*, are now mainly used for topiary, mostly when creating animals.

TOPIARY *never fails to attract attention, whether neatly and symmetrically in the form of balls, pyramids, cones or spirals, or when depicting peacocks or other animals. It is an age-old craft, frequently creating a cottage-garden aura.*

1. CREATE *a topiary squirrel by selecting a young, bushy Box plant with several pliable stems. It is possible to begin with a rooted cutting, but takes several years longer.*

2. BEND *two pieces of galvanized-wire to form the head and tail. Tie them to the plant's main stems. Clip central shoots to encourage bushiness, but allow others to develop.*

3. TIE *in body and tail shoots to the wire, at the same time regularly but lightly clipping back the young growths to encourage the development of a dense covering of leaves.*

FORMATION TRAINING

There are several secrets to success with topiary:

- Select sturdy plants, well clothed with leaves and stems. If a plant's base is bare at this stage, it will always appear unsightly.
- Start the training as soon as plants are large enough.
- Encourage the development of strong, vigorous growth during the early years.
- Above all, be patient. It may take four or more years to produce simple box outline when using Shrubby Honeysuckle (*Lonicera nitida*) or Dwarf Box (*Buxus sempervirens* 'Elegantissima'), also known as Edging Box. Creating the same feature in Yew (*Taxus baccata*) could take twice that time.

GETTING STARTED

As a novice, do not be over ambitious; it is far better to produce a pyramid or rabbit successfully than to make a mess of a giraffe!

To create a simple shape – such as a pyramid, cone, sphere or cube – begin with a single, bushy plant with healthy, strong stems and allow them to grow unchecked until 20–30cm/8–12in high. Shrubs such as the Shrubby Honeysuckle and Privet will achieve this by mid-summer during their first year of growth after being planted. Cut these shoots back by half.

As sideshoots develop, clip these shoots back by half. Repeatedly clip the vertical shoots by a third to half when the new growth is 15–20cm/6–8in long.

Continue to trim the plant in this way, to broaden and thicken it as well as to create strong, upright growth.

After about five trimmings, the plant will be bushy and ready to be cut into the desired shape. Use sharp shears.

TOPIARY *has been taken up all around the world. There is a topiary elephant at Ayutthaya in Thailand.*

PRUNING CLIMBERS

MOST climbers need to be pruned at some time, either to restrain their growth or encourage the development of flowers.

Deciduous climbers grown for their handsome foliage need little pruning, other than occasionally restricting their size.

Evergreen climbers such as ivies also need little attention. Flowering climbers, however, are the ones that need regular pruning to encourage the development of flowers. Flowering wall shrubs also need regular attention.

A TO Z OF PRUNING CLIMBERS AND WALL SHRUBS

- *Actinidia chinensis* (Chinese Gooseberry): Thin out and restrict growth in late winter.
- *Actinidia kolomikta* (Kolomikta Vine): Restrict growth during late winter.
- *Akebia:* Thin out and shorten straggly shoots in late winter.
- *Berberidopsis corallina* (Coral Plant): Thin out overcrowded shrubs in late winter.
- *Clematis macropetala:* In spring, cut out dead and thin shoots.
- *Clematis montana* (Mountain Clematis): Cut out old flowering stems in mid-summer.
- *Clematis flammula:* In late winter to early spring, cut back all shoots that flowered during the previous year to healthy buds near their bases. Also, cut out all weak and dead shoots.
- *Clematis orientalis* (Orange Peel Clematis): As for *C. flammula.*
- *Clematis tangutica:* As for *C. flammula.*
- *Clematis* (Large-flowered): For pruning, these can be divided into two main groups.

Lanuginosa and Patens types: cut back old flowering shoots after the flowers fade. Old, neglected plants can be pruned severely in late winter, but the first crop of flowers will be lost. Examples of these includes 'Nelly Moser', 'Lasurstern', 'The President' and 'Vyvyan Pennell'.

Jackmanii and Viticella types: cut plants severely, to within 30cm/12in of the ground, in early

HERBACEOUS *climbers are not common but an eye-catching one is the Yellow-leaved Hop* (Humulus lupulus *'Aureus'). Pruning is simple: just clear away all old stems down to ground level in autumn.*

FLOWERING *climbers are ideal for clothing arches and pergolas with rich colours throughout summer. This includes the large-flowered clematis (above). Wisteria, honeysuckle and jasmine provide more subtle colour.*

CLIMBERS *with evergreen, variegated leaves – such as some small and large-leafed ivies – create colour throughout the year. Other climbers have richly-coloured leaves in autumn and early winter which brighten the garden.*

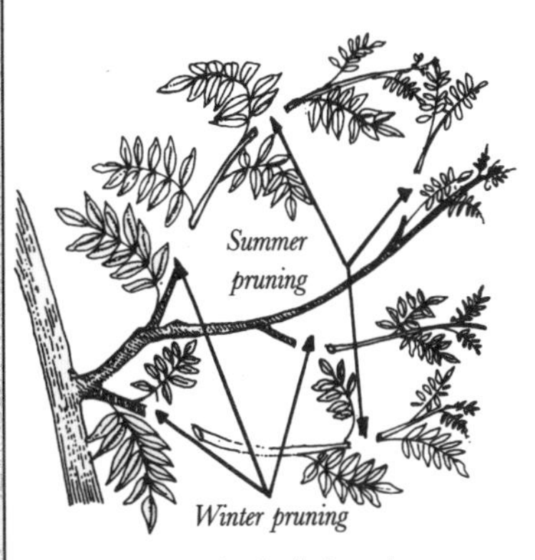

PRUNE *wisterias in late winter, cutting back sideshoots to just beyond the second leaf. Additionally, to control the growth of large, vigorous specimens, cut sideshoots back to three or four leaves during the latter part of mid-summer.*

spring. Examples of these includes 'Ernest Markham', 'Mrs Cholmondely' and 'Ville de Lyon'.

• *Eccremocarpus scaber* (Chilean Glory Flower): Cut out any frost-damaged shoots in late spring.
• *Hedera* (ivies): If necessary, prune in spring to restrain growth.
• *Humulus lupulus* 'Aureus' (Yellow-leaved Hop): Cut down and remove old shoots in autumn.
• *Hydrangea petiolaris* (Climbing Hydrangea): No regular pruning needed other than cutting out dead shoots in spring.
• *Jasminum nudiflorum* (Winter-flowering Jasmine): After flowering, cut back flowered shoots to 5–7.5cm/2–3in of their bases. Also, remove old and weak shoots.
• *Jasminum officinale* (Common White Jasmine): After the flowers fade, thin out shoots to their bases.
• *Lonicera* (Honeysuckle): No regular pruning needed, other than occasionally thinning out old shoots after the flowers fade.
• *Parthenocissus:* No regular pruning needed, other than cutting out dead or overcrowded shoots in spring to tidy them up.
• *Passiflora caerulea* (Passion Flower): In late winter, cut out tangled shoots to soil level or their bases. At the same time, cut back sideshoots to about 15cm/6in of the main stems.
• *Polygonum baldschuanicum* (Russian Vine/Bukhara Fleece Flower): Trim back large plants in spring.
• *Solanum crispum* (Chilean Potato Tree): Prune back the previous season's growth in mid-spring to 15cm/6in long. Also, cut out weak and frost-damaged shoots.
• *Vitis coignetiae* (Crimson Glory Vine): No regular pruning needed.
• *Wisteria:* See above left. Prune in winter and in summer.

TREE-LIKE WISTERIA

Wisteria is usually grown over a pergola or against a wall, but it can be trained to form a clear stem about 1.8m/6ft high and with branches trained over wires or a wooden framework.

Support a young wisteria with a strong stake and secure the stem. Cut sideshoots off when a few leaves long. When the plant reaches 45–60cm/1½–2ft above the desired height, sever it and allow sideshoots at the top to develop. Later, cut off the lower ones close to the stem.

EARLY-FLOWERNG DECIDUOUS SHRUBS

DECIDUOUS shrubs flowering in spring and early to mid-summer are some of the most richly coloured of all woody garden plants. The spring-flowering ones bloom as soon as winter disappears, with early summer-flowering types soon after them and many lasting into mid-summer.

PHILOSOPHY OF PRUNING

The time of the year when shrubs are pruned is dictated solely by the weather and the time of year when a shrub flowers.

In areas where frosts are unknown, clearly the weather is not an influence and plants can be pruned immediately they finish flowering. In other places, low temperatures have a strong influence, and a sufficiently long period must be left for fresh shoots that inevitably develop after a shrub is pruned to grow and ripen before the onset of cold weather. If insufficient time is left, tender shoots are killed in winter.

In areas where the time of pruning is dictated by the weather, shrubs are grouped into three main flowering periods:

- Spring to mid-summer flowering deciduous shrubs that flower on stems produced during the previous season. These are pruned immediately flowering ends.
- Late summer and early autumn-flowering deciduous shrubs that flower on stems produced earlier in the same season. These are pruned during spring or early summer of the following year (see pages 24 and 25).
- Winter-flowering deciduous shrubs. These require little pruning, other than cutting out unrequired stems in spring (see pages 26 and 27).

PREVIOUS SEASON'S WOOD

Spring-flowering shrubs, as well as those that produce their display in the early part of summer, develop flowers on stems and shoots that developed during the previous

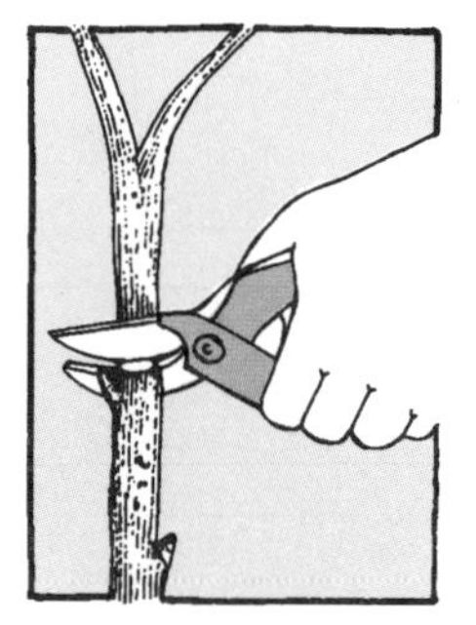

1. USE *sharp secateurs to cut slightly above a healthy, outward-pointing bud. This helps to create a shrub with an open centre where light and air can penetrate to ripen young shoots.*

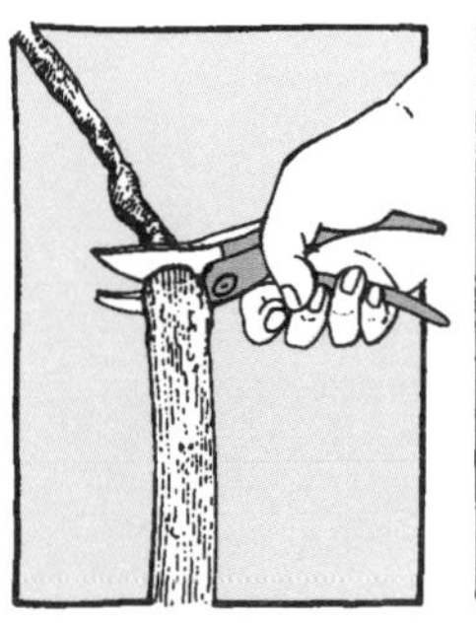

2. CUT *out dead or damaged shoots, severing them just above a bud. Shoots die from many reasons, including frost, pest and diseases. Immature stems are easily killed.*

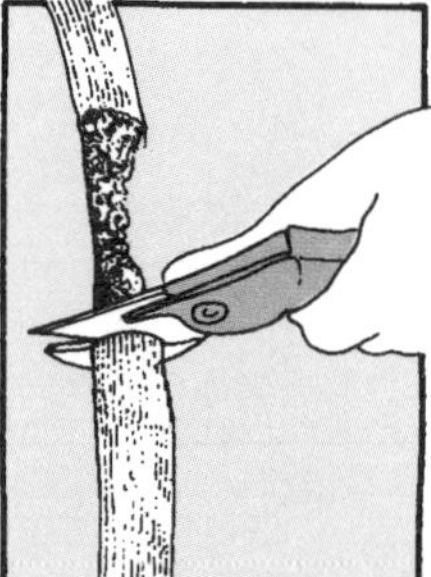

3. CUT *out diseased stems, cutting slightly above a bud. These are likely to occur when shrubs have centres congested with stems. If left, they encourage the spread of disease to all parts.*

year. The precise time when they flower is strongly influenced by the local climate and duration of winter. Indeed, flowering may vary by four weeks or even more in latitudes only five hundred miles apart.

These shrubs are pruned immediately their flowers fade, cutting back flowered shoots to fresh young growths. During the remaining part of summer and early autumn these will develop into shoots that bear flowers during the following year.

If pruning is neglected, plants soon become congested. Also, new shoots remain thin and spindly and the quality of flowers dramatically decreases.

LIGHT AND AIR

At the same time as cutting out shoots that have just borne flowers, remove:

- Thin and spindly shoots: if left, they are an eyesore and never bear satisfactory flowers.
- Shoots that cross the shrub's centre: these restrict the flow of air through the shrub and encourage the presence of diseases. They also reduce the amount of light, which prevents stems ripening properly before the onset of cold winter weather.
- Damaged shoots: if left, these encourage the presence of pests and diseases.
- Pest-ridden and diseased shoots: if left, they spread infection.

BALANCED GROWTH

As well as encouraging a shrub to develop a good display of flowers, pruning also ensures that it is growing evenly and not lop-sided. Inevitably, after a few years a shrub develops a thick base and it may be necessary to cut out old stems. When this is done it often results in imbalanced growth. Therefore, take this into consideration and remove stems from the other side of the shrub as well.

SHRUBS PRUNED IN THIS WAY INCLUDE:

- Golden Bells *(Forsythia)*
- Mock Orange *(Philadelphus)*
- Flowering Currant *(Ribes)*

MOCK ORANGE AND LILAC

Mock Orange (Philadelphus), *below, is often erroneously called* Syringa *because it was introduced into Europe at about the same time as lilac, now botanically known as* Syringa. *Initially, they were thought to have features in common – hollow, pithy wood that could be made into pipes.*

BILLHOOKS *have been used for centuries, either for harvesting plants or crudely pruning them. Here is an industrious harvester from a German calendar, of 1487.*

LATE SUMMER-FLOWERING SHRUBS

These are richly-flowered shrubs that brighten borders in late summer and frequently into early autumn. Their growth is curtailed by the onset of cold weather during early winter.

Unlike shrubs that flower early in the year, late summer-flowering ones develop their flowers on shoots produced earlier in the same year. They are therefore pruned in spring as soon as all risk of cold weather damaging young shoots has passed.

The time when the risk of frost has passed depends on the locality and latitude. Some places may seldom have frosts, while others still experience them in late spring and early summer. It is, therefore, essential to be guided by the weather pattern in your area, rather than by a fixed date that cannot, in all cases, be right.

SEVERE PRUNING

Many late summer-flowering shrubs respond to being cut back severely to fresh, young shoots near their bases. Because these shrubs develop vigorous shoots within a few months they must be grown in fertile soil.

Crossing and twiggy shoots must be cut out, in the same way as when pruning spring and early summer-flowering types.

SHRUBS PRUNED IN THIS WAY INCLUDE:

- Butterfly Bush *(Buddleia davidii)*
- Californian Lilacs (deciduous types, such as *Ceanothus* 'Gloire de Versailles' and *Ceanothus* 'Topaz')
- Tamarix/Tamarisk *(Tamarix pentandra)*

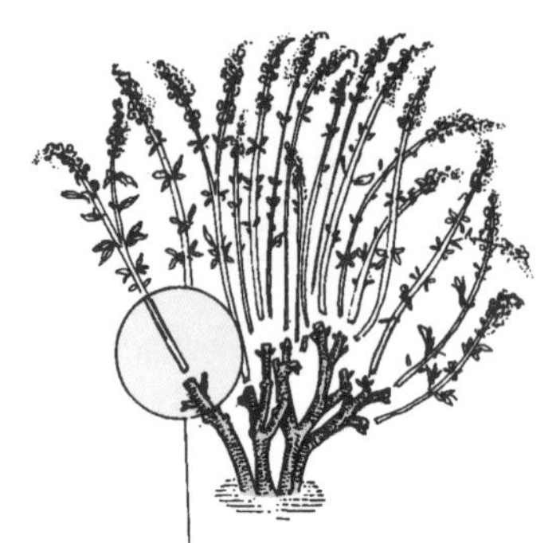

1. CUT *flowered stems back to outward-pointing buds to ensure plants grow outwards and develop open centres, through which air can penetrate and light enter to ripen shoots.*

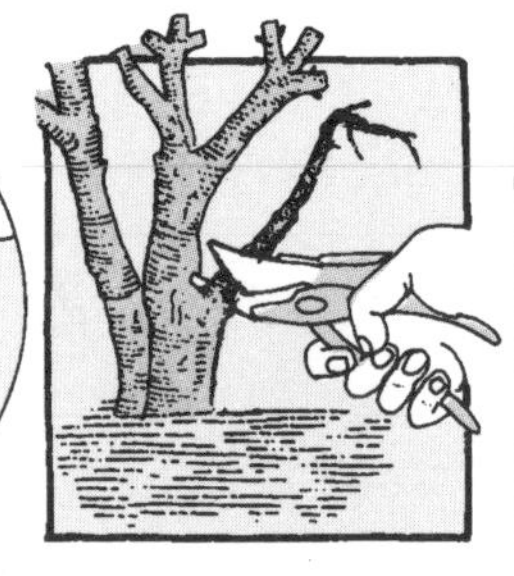

2. EVERY *year, cut out a few old shoots to their bases to encourage the development of others. This is essential to ensure shrubs eventually do not become full of old stems at their bases.*

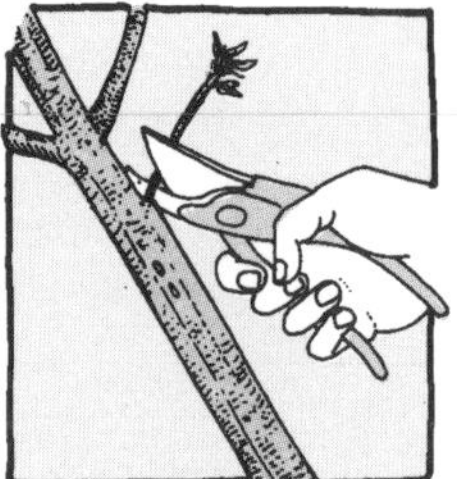

3. CUT *out twiggy stems close to their bases. If left, they congest the centres of plants, reducing air circulation and encouraging the avoidable presence of pests and diseases.*

QUEST FOR PLANTS

Early in man's development, plants were mainly prized for their food or medicinal value. Later, spices and herbs became desirable as ways to cloak the incipient decay in an increasingly wide range of food. Indeed, in Europe it was the denial of essential spices from the Spice Islands in eastern Indonesia that triggered the westward search and Christopher Columbus's chancing on the shores of North America.

The Romans spread food and herb plants throughout Europe, but they also appreciated plants solely for their beauty. Indeed, Cleopatra, in about 50 BC, is said to have seduced Mark Antony on a bed of rose petals. At the same time, the Romans imported roses from Alexandria in North Africa.

EARLY HERBALS

Plants were recorded and discussed by Roman botanists, but it was not until the invention of moveable type in Germany in 1440 that there began a wider interest in herbals and plants.

By 1600, plant nurseries were established and in 1601 and 1609 the French nurseryman Jean Robin issued catalogues of plants, some from North America. In England, in 1605, James I granted a Royal Charter to the Company of Gardeners which banned the sale of poor-quality plants.

With an increased demand for new plants, there was a tremendous impetus in many countries for nurseries and botanic gardens to send botanists and gardeners abroad to bring back new plants.

Spain, France, Holland, Sweden and England were prominent in creating botanic gardens and sending out botanists and plant hunters. Trading institutions such as the East India Company and Dutch East India Company also helped in plant exploration.

The first crossing of North America in search of plants was made by Captains Merriweather Lewis and William Clark in 1804. They started from St. Louis and reached the Columbia River, on the borders of what are now the states of Washington and Oregon. One of the areas rich in plants was China, but its borders remained closed to foreigners, even in the mid-eighteenth century. North America, however, was freely open and many shrubs and trees from there have been spread throughout the world.

CREATING A BUTTERFLY GARDEN

The Butterfly Bush (Buddleia davidii) *is, perhaps, the best known shrub that attracts butterflies. Its long, pyramidal flower heads, in a range of colours including white, violet-blue, reddish-purple or blue, are attractive when peppered with butterflies. Other shrubs that attract butterflies include lavender, lilac, Privet and Alder Buckthorn* (Rhamnus frangula).

WINTER-FLOWERING SHRUBS

THESE are the easiest of all deciduous shrubs to prune. They appear to burst into flower each winter, regardless of what is done to them, but there are several basic pruning techniques that will prolong their lives for many years. Deciduous winter-flowering shrubs usually flower on short, leafless spurs that arise from the main branches. These increase slightly in size each year, but not noticeably and the shrub therefore appears to remain the same size for many years. In reality, this is wrong as a young witch hazel planted when 90cm/3ft high will, after about twenty years, be three or more times that height. Nevertheless, unlike late summer-flowering shrubs, where growth is dominant and a large part of the shrub removed each spring, the winter-flowering types have a less vigorous nature.

REGULAR PRUNING

Like all other shrubs, winter-flowering types are equally likely to have damaged shoots, either physically or from diseases.

Exceptionally cold winters sometimes injure unripened shoot tips, while those that rub against each other create damaged areas susceptible to diseases. Such areas may also occur as a result of insect and bird damage during summer.

CUTTING OUT IN SPRING

Damaged areas must be cut out in spring, but not before all risk of severe frosts has passed. Always cut stems back to healthy buds; this is usually possible when trimming damaged shoot tips, but if a diseased area occurs on an old shoot this may not be possible.

Thin, twiggy shoots growing towards the plant's centre must be cut out before they develop into large branches. An open centre to the shrub encourages air to circulate freely, as well as light to enter

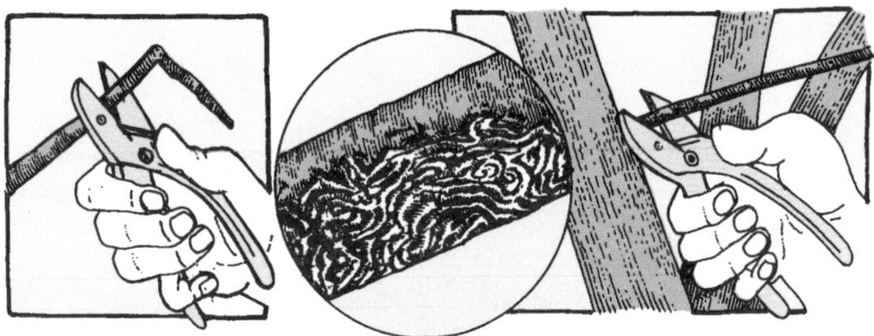

1. IN *spring, cut back damaged shoot tips (above) to healthy, outward-growing buds. This is usually only necessary in exceptionally cold areas, and even then it only generally occurs on unripened, young, immature shoots.*

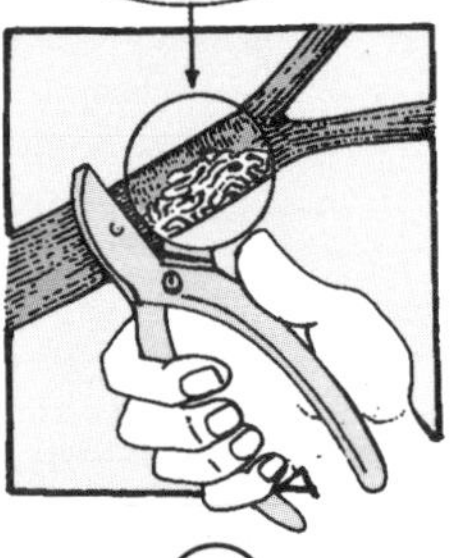

2. CUT *out (left) diseased areas. If left, they eventually girdle the stem and cause it to die. Insect pests, as well as birds, cause injuries that encourage the presence of diseases. Also, cut out all twiggy and crossing shoots (above).*

WITCH HAZELS

These are superb deciduous shrubs for brightening winter. The Chinese Witch Hazel (Hamamelis mollis), *pictured here, has sweetly-scented, deep-yellow, strap-like petals. It is, however, the bark of the North American* Hamamelis virginiana *that produces the well-known, medicinal witch hazel. It flowers earlier than other witch hazels and is variously known as the Common Witch Hazel, Spotted Alder and Winter Bloom. Its bark provides an astringent liquid frequently employed as an antiseptic and skin cleanser. It has also been used as a tonic and sedative and is most valuable in checking internal and external haemorrhages. Long before Christopher Columbus chanced upon the New World, the Indians used its inner bark for external applications to treat sore eyes, tumours and inflammations.*

to ripen young wood in summer. Also, branches that are allowed to develop in the plant's centre may, eventually, rub on other shoots and cause damage.

RESTRICTING SIZE

All shrubs ought to be selected to suit a particular position in a garden, so that drastic, size-diminishing pruning is not eventually needed. In the real world, however, this does not always happen and some shrubs eventually require quite extensive and severe pruning.

Fortunately, it is easier to restrain the size – within reason – of winter-flowering shrubs than any others. This is because each year they put on less growth than most types.

When restricting its size, do not imbalance the shape and create a lop-sided specimen. This is not only quite unpleasant to the eye, but puts extra strain on the main stem and increases the chance of wind loosening the plant.

Always cut stems back to other shoots: leaving stubs is unsightly and encourages the presence of diseases. If cuts are large, pare them smooth with a sharp knife and cover with a fungicidal tree paint to stop infection.

THE *Winter Sweet* (Chimonanthus praecox *'Grandiflorus') has spicy-scented flowers from mid to late winter. It is ideal for planting alongside paths, where it creates a wonderful aroma.*

SHRUBS PRUNED IN THIS WAY INCLUDE:

- Chinese Witch Hazel *(Hamamelis mollis)*
- Cornelian Cherry *(Cornus mas)*
- Japanese Witch Hazel *(Hamamelis japonica)*
- Ozark Witch Hazel *(Hamamelis vernalis)*
- Winter-flowering Viburnums (*Viburnum farreri/fragrans, V. grandiflorum, V. x bodnantense* 'Dawn' and *V. x bodnantense* 'Deben')

DECIDUOUS TREES

DECIDUOUS trees need very little pruning, but as they are long-lived it is essential to create an evenly-shaped, attractive outline when young.

Part of the initial training and pruning is to ensure the trunk is upright and this is achieved by regularly checking the stake and tie securing it. The top of the stake should be just below the crotch, with the tree secured to it by two proprietary tree ties. For standard trees, with long trunks, use three tree ties. These need to be checked every few months in summer to ensure the trunk is not constricted. Proprietary, plastic types are easily adjusted as the trunk ages and broadens.

WELL-SPACED STEMS

There should be three or four well-spaced stems growing from the top of the trunk – eventually they will form the main branches. Cut off shoots growing inwards from these main stems to ensure that the tree's centre is open.

If the ends of shoots are damaged, cut back to a healthy, upward pointing buds.

PRUNE WHEN DORMANT

Most pruning of deciduous trees is performed in winter, when dormant. But flowering cherries and other members of the Prunus family are best pruned in late spring or early summer when the sap begins to rise. This is because disease spores are less likely to enter cuts when the tree's sap is rising.

If pruning in late spring or early summer means cutting off a large amount of blossom, prune in late summer instead.

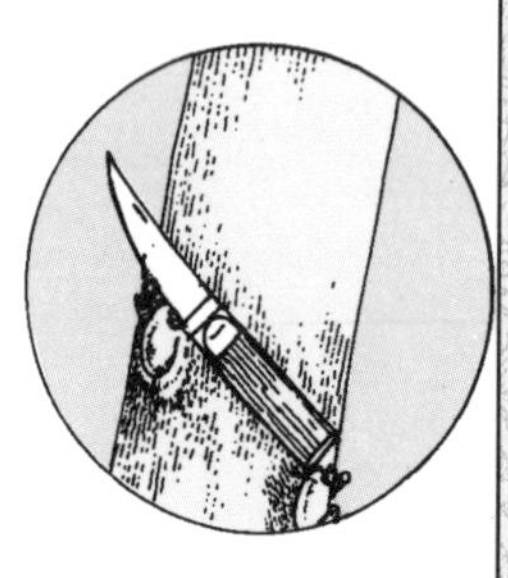

1. WATER-SHOOTS *frequently appear on established trees and mar their appearance. They also sap the tree's energy, which otherwise would be directed into growth, leaves and flowers. They appear on trunks and major branches.*

2. USE *a sharp saw to cut the shoots close to the trunk or branch. Normal saws are often impossible to use between congested shoots. A curved Grecian saw that cuts on the pull stroke is the best type to use in constricted places on trunks.*

3. USE *a sharp knife to smooth the cut ends level with the trunk. Do not make the area larger than necessary as this may encourage the development of further water-shoots. Cover large areas with a fungicidal paint.*

TREE DOCTORING

Trees are part of our heritage and occasionally some need help to see them through to old age. From infancy, many branches naturally droop, the weight of the branch itself and foliage forever bearing downwards.

Branches are easily supported by fixing stout, metal or wooden props under them. This has the advantage of being independent of the rest of the tree. Alternatively, hooks are bolted into the branch, which is then suspended from a branch higher up and towards the tree's centre. Whatever the method, it must not constrict the branch.

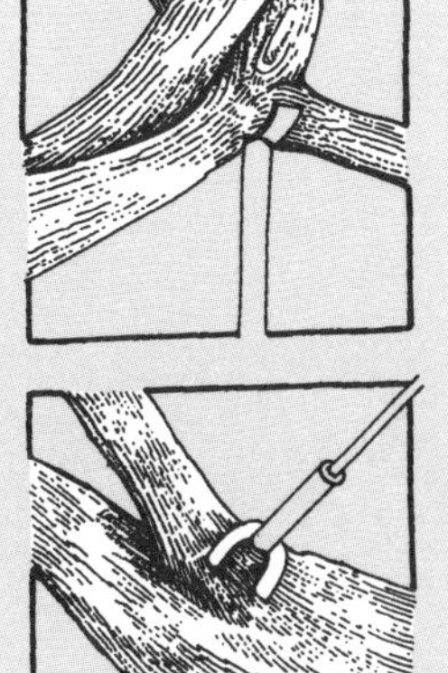

SUPPORT *large branches (above) either with metal or wooden props, positioned on a firm base, or by a large hook drilled into the branch and secured by nuts and washers. A cable secured to a higher branch can then be used to hold it in position.*

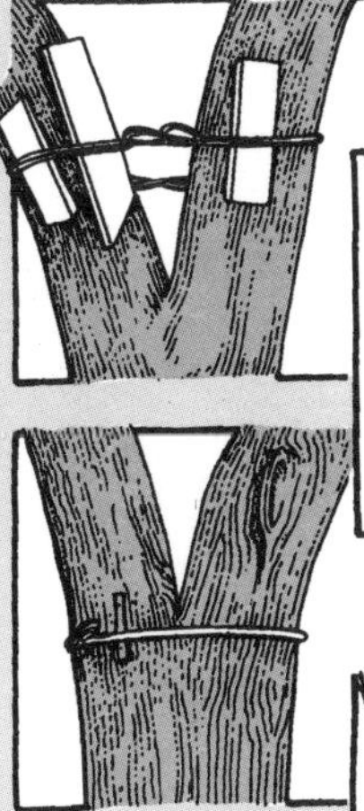

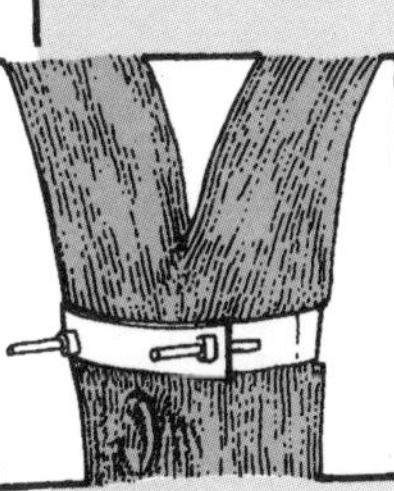

1. THE *three ways (above) to prevent branches splitting and tearing the trunk are initially effective, but after a few years cut into the bark and constrict growth. Even placing wood to form a pad between the wire and tree restricts growth after a few years of active growth.*

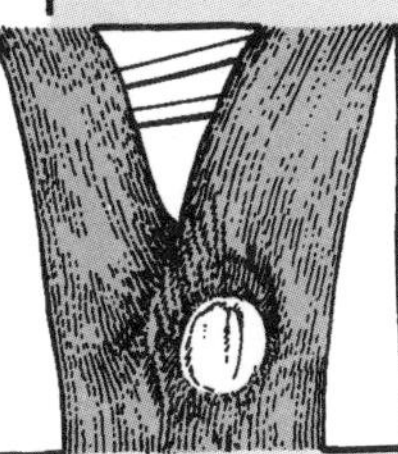

2. BRACE *split trunks with threaded rods inserted through drilled holes and secured at their ends with large washers and nuts. Ensure that the washers are large, so that they are not forced into the bark when the nuts are tightened at the ends of the rods.*

FILLING CAVITIES

Large, old trees often have cavities that if left untreated cause the entire trunk to decay.

- *Remove dead and diseased wood. Scrape the area back to sound, healthy and firm timber.*
- *Paint the area with a wood preservative. Allow to dry and cover with a thick coating of a bituminous compound.*
- *Create a drainage channel by boring a hole from the lowest point to the outside.*
- *Fill up the whole area with cement – level with the inner bark.*

EVERGREEN SHRUBS

EVERGREEN shrubs, unlike deciduous types, are clothed in leaves all year round, although they regularly drop them throughout the year. Most leaves live for at least one full year before falling.

Once established, evergreen shrubs usually need no more attention than to shape them and cut out weak, diseased and straggly shoots in spring. In cold areas, leave this job until early summer.

AVOID WINTER PRUNING

It is essential not to prune evergreens in winter, as any young shoots that develop after pruning will be killed and may mean that pruning has to be carried out again to remove unsightly shoots and to encourage the development of further ones.

DELAY UNTIL AFTER FLOWERING

If the evergreen shrub blooms in spring, delay pruning until the flowers have completely died. Examples of this are Darwin's Berberis *(Berberis darwinii)* and *Berberis x stenophylla.*

ROOM DECORATION

*Evergreen shrubs with variegated leaves are ideal for including in floral arrangements indoors – especially in winter when there is a dearth of colourful flowers available. The Spotted Laurel (*Aucuba japonica *'Variegata') is popular with flower arrangers.*

Always cut shoots from the back of a shrub and in several different places, rather than from one position. Also, sever each stem just above a leaf joint.

MAJOR SURGERY

Sometimes, major surgery is needed when evergeens become too large and spreading. This is best tackled as soon as growth begins in spring so as to allow as long a period as possible for young growths to develop before the onset of cold winter weather.

Occasionally, when evergreens are cut back dramatically, the flowers that would have developed during the season following pruning have to be sacrificed.

Remember that the further back into old wood evergreens are cut, the more difficult it is for them to develop fresh shoots.

If a neglected shrub is exceptionally old and tough, cut only a few of the old shoots back during the first season. If these produce shoots, cut back the other ones in the following season. If not successful, cut them less far into the older wood.

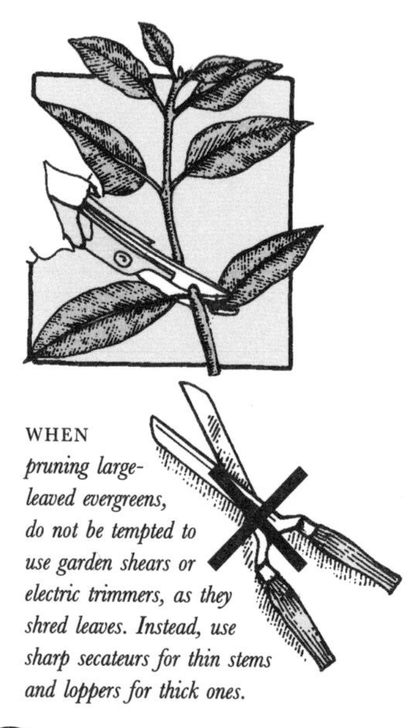

WHEN *pruning large-leaved evergreens, do not be tempted to use garden shears or electric trimmers, as they shred leaves. Instead, use sharp secateurs for thin stems and loppers for thick ones.*

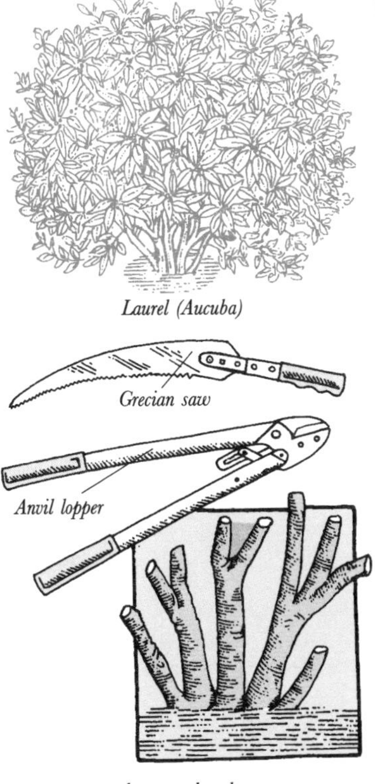

MANY *large, neglected, evergreen shrubs eventually dominate gardens. They can, however, be given a new lease of life by cutting them back to their bases in spring.*

PRUNING EVERGREEN CONIFERS

A few conifers, such as larixes and the Maidenhair Tree *(Ginkgo biloba)*, are deciduous, but most are evergreen and create attractive screens and features throughout the year. Conifers – as well as other trees with sappy wood, such as birch, Horse Chestnut and some maples – bleed profusely when pruned in spring and summer. These are therefore best cut in late autumn or early winter when there is not an active flow of sap. It gives cuts ample time to heal before spring.

PICKING TEA LEAVES

Few people have not drunk tea, which is prepared from Camellia thea, *a relative of the much desired* Camellia japonica *that adorns gardens in late winter and spring.*

Tea was grown in China as early as 2700 BC *and there is a Japanese legend that China is its home, although it has never been found in a wild state in that country. It has, however, been discovered growing wild in the forests of Assam in eastern India and it is conceivable that Chinese traders travelled there to obtain seeds of the precious plant.*

For a long time, India remained unaware of the treasure bestowed by nature on her doorstep and started cultivating tea by importing seeds from China. Records indicate that Assam Tea was introduced into Ceylon (now Sri Lanka) in 1839, and from China in 1824.

Picking – or plucking as it is widely termed – both provides the source of tea and prunes the bushes so that they develop further sideshoots. The best tea is obtained by 'fine plucking', when the leading shoot and two leaves are removed. 'Coarse plucking' yields lower-quality tea and is when the leading shoots and four leaves are removed.

When the bushes stop producing leaves (known as flushing) they are pruned back severely. In warm, low lands this is performed every sixteen to twenty months, but at higher elevations it is carried out every three years.

SHRUBS WITH COLOURED STEMS

Several shrubs are grown for their coloured stems, which look especially attractive in winter. When planted around a pond they reflect in the pool's surface.

To encourage these suckering shrubs to develop attractive, stems, cut the complete plant down to within about 7.5cm/3in of the ground in mid-spring. This drastic pruning encourages the development of fresh shoots.

Repeated hard pruning eventually creates plants with masses of stubby shoots at their bases. This need not be a problem, as fresh shoots soon grow.

Because each year these shrubs develop a complete new array of stems and leaves, they need to be planted in rich, moisture-retentive soil. In poor, dry soils they do not create a good display.

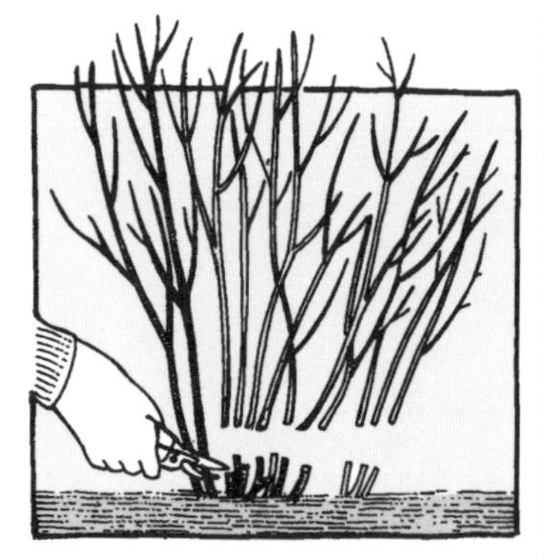

CUT *stems of dogwoods to within 7.5cm/3in of the ground in mid-spring to encourage fresh ones.*

SHRUBS WITH COLOURED STEMS INCLUDE:

- *Cornus alba* (Red-barked Dogwood). Red stems.
- *Cornus alba* 'Kesselringii'. Purplish-black stems.
- *Cornus alba* 'Sibirica' (Westonbirt Dogwood). Bright crimson stems.
- *Cornus stolonifera* 'Flaviramea'. Young shoots yellow to olive-green in winter.

DEAD-HEADING RHODODEDRONS

Large-flower rhododendrons benefit from having their dead flowers removed. This encourages development of further shoots, rather than seeds.

After the flowers fade, snap the stem just below the old flower-head, while holding the stem firmly.

PRUNE *Mop-headed Hydrangeas (left) every year. Cut off dead flower-heads immediately after flowering in late summer. Alternatively, leave the flower-heads on the plants until spring – they look attractive in winter when covered with frost.*

In spring, cut out thin, weak and damaged shoots, as well as a few two- or three-year-old stems to encourage the development of fresh, strong, young ones. Do not shorten young, vigorous shoots as they may have dormant flower-buds.

HEATHERS AND HEATHS

Callunas, ericas and daboecias are kept tidy and with a neat outline by lightly trimming them with hedging shears. Do not use secateurs, as these do not allow contoured outlines to be created.

HEATHERS *and heaths are best clipped with hedging shears, removing old flower heads and creating a neat, attractive, undulating outline.*

CALLUNAS AND SUMMER-FLOWERING ERICAS

Trim callunas and summer-flowering ericas in spring. Use hedging shears to trim off dead flowers and to create a neat, undulating outline. Ensure this job is tackled before growth starts in spring, as otherwise young shoots that would bear flowers later in the season are clipped off.

Plants pruned in this way:

- Bell Heather/Twisted Heather *(Erica cinerea)*
- Cornish Heath *(Erica vagans)*
- Corsican Heath *(Erica terminalis)*
- Cross-leaved Heath *(Erica tetralix)*
- Heather/Scotch Heather/Ling *(Calluna vulgaris)*

WINTER AND SPRING-FLOWERING TYPES

These are trimmed after they finish flowering, again lightly cutting off dead flower-heads and creating a pleasing outline.

Do not leave the trimmings on the plants: brush them off with a soft broom.

Plants pruned in this way:

- Heather *(Erica x darleyensis)*
- Mediterranean Heather *(Erica mediterranea/E. hibernica)*
- Spring Heather/Snow Heather *(Erica herbacea/E. carnea)*

DABOECIAS

Use hedging shears to trim off old flower heads and the loose ends of shoots in late autumn, after flowering has finished. In cold areas, leave this job until early spring.

Plants pruned in this way:

- St. Dabeoc's Heath/Irish Heath *(Daboecia cantabrica)*

TREE HEATHS

These need little pruning, other than shortening long ends of straggly shoots in late spring after the flowers fade. Also, remove straggly shoots to maintain an even and attractive shape.

Plants pruned in this way:

- Tree Heath *(Erica arborea)*
- Spanish Heath/Portugal Heath *(Erica lusitanica)*

BRIAR PIPES

*The roots of the Tree Heath (*Erica arborea*) were widely used in southern France and the Iberian Peninsula to make pipes for smoking tobacco. Briar is in fact a corruption of the French word for heather, 'bruyère'.*

PRUNING ROSES

REGULARLY and systematically pruning roses is relatively new and dates back only to the middle of the nineteenth century. It did not develop into a technique until the introduction of hybrid teas in 1867, although the hybrid perpetuals that reached the peak of their development slightly earlier were also regularly pruned. Before then, roses were not highly considered as shrubs for borders and the only treatment they were given was thinning: cutting out dead or overcrowded shoots.

Nowadays, the purpose of pruning is to encourage the yearly production of healthy, well-sized flowers on plants that have a long lifespan. It is an essential part of growing roses, but regrettably too often steeped in mysticism.

MYSTICISM REMOVED

If one considers that hybrid tea and floribunda roses – by far the most popular of all bush roses – are just vigorous, deciduous shrubs that flower mainly on new shoots developed earlier in the same year, then the mysticism is removed. The other important factor is winter, as this influences the time of year when pruning is performed.

AUTUMN OR SPRING PRUNING?

Although pruning can be done at any time during a plant's dormant period, in exceptionally cold areas it is best left until early spring. There are, however, advantages of both times where temperatures are not too low.

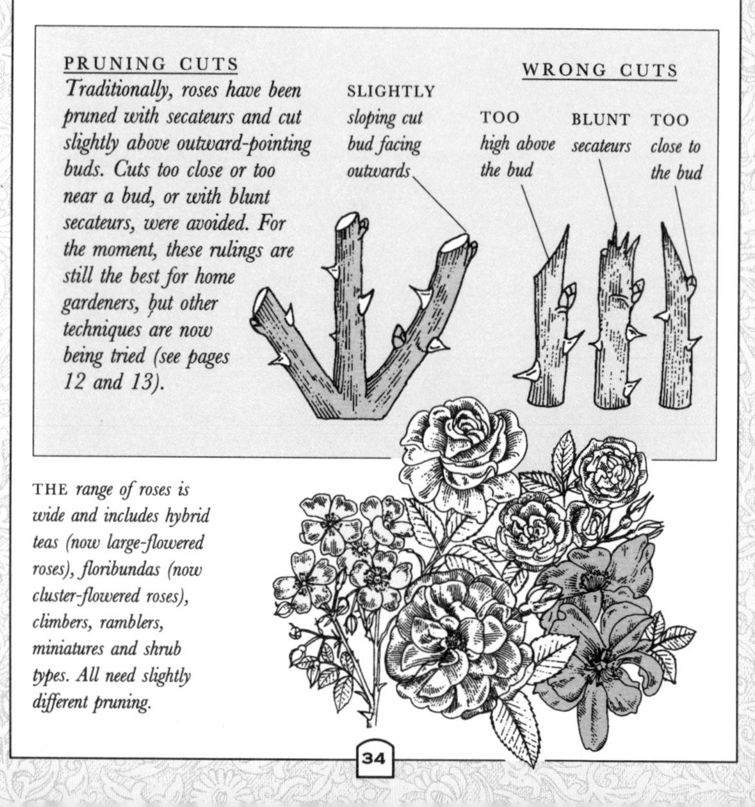

PRUNING CUTS

Traditionally, roses have been pruned with secateurs and cut slightly above outward-pointing buds. Cuts too close or too near a bud, or with blunt secateurs, were avoided. For the moment, these rulings are still the best for home gardeners, but other techniques are now being tried (see pages 12 and 13).

THE *range of roses is wide and includes hybrid teas (now large-flowered roses), floribundas (now cluster-flowered roses), climbers, ramblers, miniatures and shrub types. All need slightly different pruning.*

TRADITIONALLY, *roses have been planted as 'bare-rooted' plants. Before planting bush roses, cut back stems of hybrid teas to about 15cm/6in long, and floribundas to 20–23cm/8–9in. Additionally, cut out weak, twiggy and inward-growing shoots. Shorten long roots to about 30cm/12in, and cut out damaged ones. Before planting, immerse the roots in water overnight. Plants with dry roots take longer to become established.*

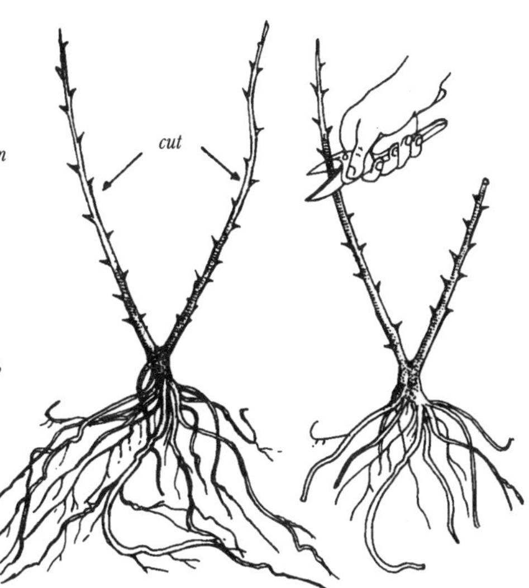

Pruning in autumn makes diseased shoots easier to see and remove, as well as other shoots from the plant's base. Also, because diseased shoots are removed early there is less chance of spores being carried over to another year.

Pruning in autumn removes much of a plant's top growth and thereby reduces the area that can be battered by strong winter winds that may loosen roots in the soil. However, even if pruning is left until spring, long shoots can be cut off in autumn and the risk of root disturbance diminished.

If roses are pruned in autumn there is a chance that young, newly-formed shoots may be damaged by cold winter weather: pruning in spring reduces this risk. Also, by leaving pruning until spring, it is possible to enjoy the attractive fruits (hips or heps) of some rose species when there is a dearth of interest in a garden.

DEAD-HEADING

Cutting off dead flowers from hybrid tea and floribunda roses encourages further blooms. Cut slightly above the second or third leaf below the dead flower head.

DISBUDDING

Performed on hybrid tea roses to produce larger blooms.

REMOVING SUCKER SHOOTS

Because most roses are budded and therefore do not grow on their own roots, sucker shoots often develop from ground level. Remove them as soon as they are seen, but do not cut them off as this encourages even more shoots. Instead, dig down around the sucker and pull it off. Wear strong gloves when tackling this job.

If removing suckers is neglected, they eventually dominate the plant. Shoots also appear on the stems of standard and half-standard roses. Rub them off as soon as you see them.

HYBRID TEA AND FLORIBUNDA ROSES

If you ask twelve rose experts how to prune a bush rose you would probably get a dozen different answers. As well as considering the basic technique they would take thought about the soil, vigour of the variety and weather pattern in their locality. Here, however, we first present the basic philosophy, later highlighting a few other considerations.

FROM LIGHT TO HARD
There are three basic methods of pruning: 'Light' (in some areas known as Low Pruning), 'Moderate' (also known and Medium Pruning) and 'Hard' (frequently referred to as High or Long Pruning).

All of these terms refer to the amount of wood pruned out of a plant, whether when young or

BEFORE | AFTER | TYPE

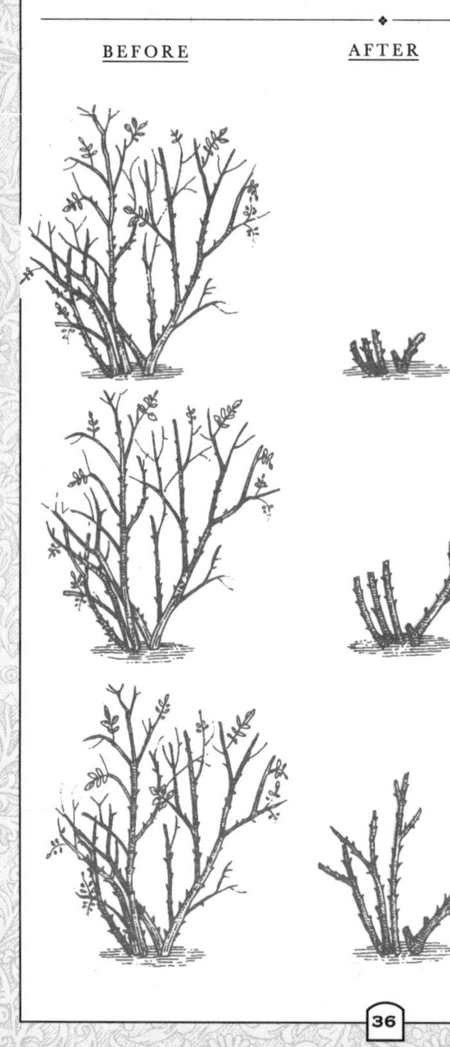

HARD PRUNING
Cut stems back to three or four buds. This is recommended for newly-planted hybrid tea and floribunda bush roses. It is only suitable for weak-growing varieties of established hybrid teas, as well those grown to produce exhibition blooms.

MODERATE PRUNING
Cut stems – whether produced from the base or lateral shoots from older wood – back to about half their length. Cut weak stems more severely. Most hybrid tea roses are pruned in this way, as well as floribundas but with a variation of old stems severely pruned.

LIGHT PRUNING
Cut stems back by removing one-third of their length. It is ideal for vigorous hybrid teas, as when pruned too hard it encourages excessive growth. It is also suitable for roses growing in light, sandy, impoverished soils.

established. And although hard pruning is recommended for both hybrid tea and floribunda roses when young, for most it is not the best way to prune established bushes. Then, most rose bushes are moderately pruned; while a few exceptionally vigorous types, as well as those on light, sandy and impoverished soils that dry out in summer, are lightly cut.

FINE TUNING
Rose varieties vary widely in their vigour: those with a weak nature are pruned harder than vigorous types. This is because the harder a shrub is pruned, the more growth it makes. Rose catalogues frequently indicate a plant's vigour. Where soils are light, exceptionally well-drained and impoverished, light pruning is recommended. However, continued light pruning over several years produces tall, spindly bushes that bear poor quality flowers.

Hybrid tea roses with flowers in shades of yellow frequently respond well to light pruning.

EXHIBITION BLOOMS
Varieties of hybrid teas grown primarily to produce exhibition blooms with long, straight stems are frequently hard pruned, although many rose experts consider this too dramatic for the long-term health of the bush.

WEEPING STANDARDS

With their pendulous growth, weeping standards have grace and elegance. Varieties with a slender, pendulous habit are budded on root-stocks 1.3–1.5m/ 4½–5ft high. A wire umbrella is secured to the top of a stout stake and the weeping stems are trained over its ribs.

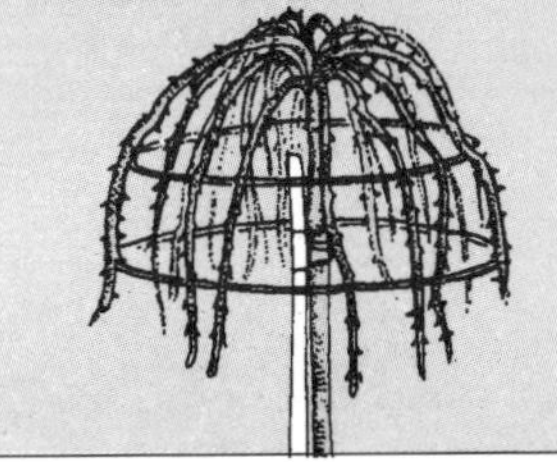

CLOSELY-PLANTED BUSHES
Where hybrid tea roses are planted close together in beds, hard pruning is often practised and consists of cutting all shoots to within 20cm/8in of the ground. It encourages strong growth.

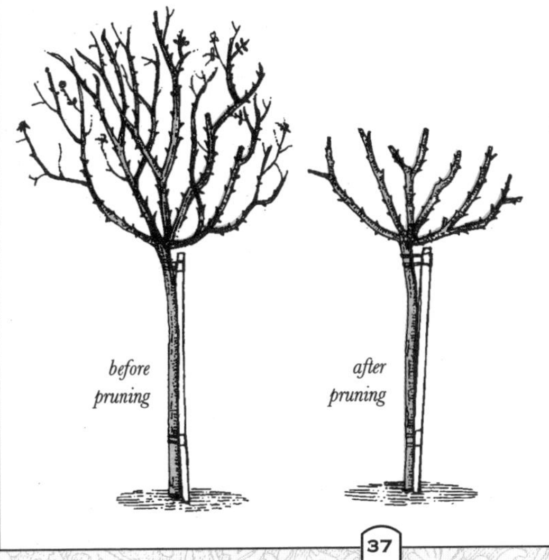

HALF- *and full-standards are superb for bringing height to borders. Half-standards are budded on a root-stock at about 75cm/2½ft above the ground, and at 1m/3½ft high for full standards. They are pruned less severely than bush types. It is essential to build up a well-balanced head. Remove dead, twiggy and congested shoots from the standard's centre.*

SHRUB ROSES

PRUNING shrub roses is important and best tackled in late winter, although any time up to the end of early spring is all right. Unlike hybrid tea and floribunda roses, which need to be pruned hard during their first year, shrub roses can be left without being pruned for the first two years after being set in the ground.

PRUNING OBJECTIVES

During their early years, allow shrub roses to build up their growth and to form strong stems. Thereafter, prune them every year, including the following:

- Cut away dead and diseased shoots. Carefully inspect around the shrub's base, where stems are often congested.
- Prune out, close to their bases, very weak and twiggy shoots.
- With age, shrub roses usually become crowded with stems: cut away to their bases very old stems so that space is left for young ones. Severely cutting back aged stems also has the advantage in encouraging the production of young shoots. The aim should be to continually initiate the formation of fresh shoots.
- Once all the old, dead and twiggy shoots are removed, there is a decision to be made about the severity of pruning the remainder of the shrub. Cutting back shoots dramatically, perhaps by a half, encourages large, high quality flowers. However, if you want masses of flowers, just lightly cut off the tips of shoots. Usually, it is better to aim for something between these two extremes.
- Roses that are true species – as well as those with a similar nature – need no pruning except the removal of dead, twiggy and diseased shoots, and an occasional thinning of old shoots.
- Often, shrub roses are allowed to scramble and sprawl into other plants. In such cases, little pruning is needed other than to remove old, dead and diseased shoots.

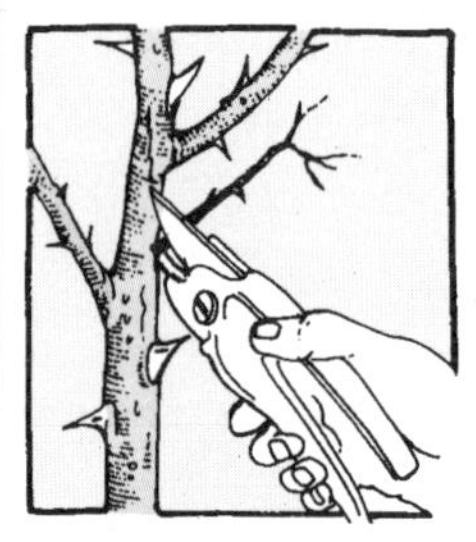

1. FROM *late winter to early spring, cut out thin, weak, twiggy and diseased shoots. This aspect of pruning is common to most roses, as well as other shrubs, but is no less important for the health and vigour of shrub roses.*

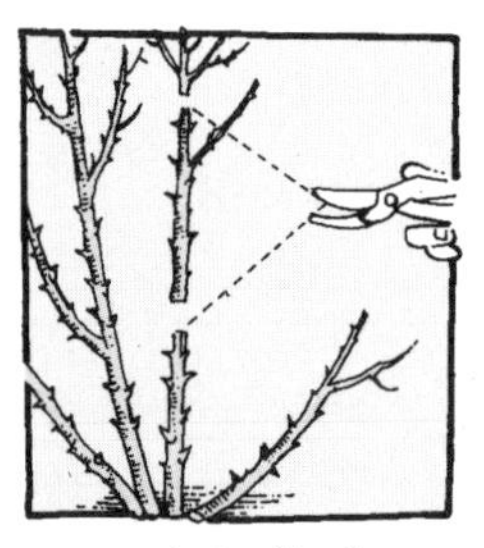

2. THE *degree of hard or light pruning dictates the amount of growth during the following year: for large, high quality flowers cut shoots back severely, perhaps by a half. Light pruning, however, creates more but smaller flowers.*

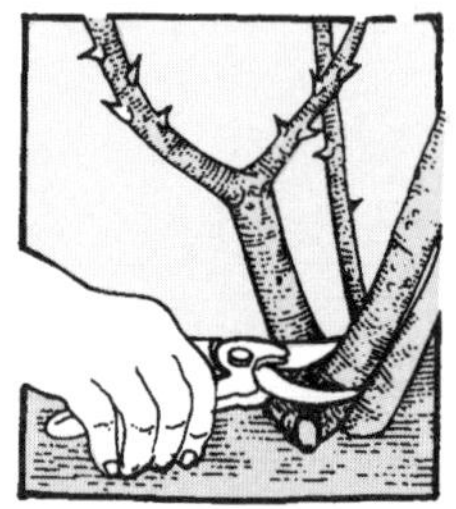

3. SHRUB *roses can even be lightly pruned so that existing stems and branches remain and fill a specified area. Nevertheless, regularly remove a few old stems from the base of the shrub to encourage the development of others and continuing beauty.*

SCENTED ROSES

Richly fragrant roses have always been prized. According to legend, it was the Indian Princess Nur-mahal and her husband, the Great Moghul, who discovered Attar of Roses. They are said to have been rowing on an ornamental canal filled with rose water and noticed that the sun's rays had separated the water from the essential oil. It was found to be an exquisite perfume.

ENGLISH ROSES

The main criticism of 'old roses' is that they usually only have one flush of flowers and that their colour range is rather limited. With this in mind, English roses have been developed. They are recurrent flowering, which means that after their first flush they continue to produce blooms, although perhaps intermittently. Also, they have a wider colour range. Their growth is usually bushy and most have a pleasing fragrance.

Because of the improved characteristics – and especially the repeat flowering – they need slightly different pruning.

The aim must be to build up a bushy plant. If you are buying from a nursery specializing in English roses, they probably will have been initially pruned before despatch and therefore no further pruning is needed during the first year. However, always cut out thin, decayed and damaged growths. During following years:

- Cut out weak and twiggy growth, as well as dead and diseased shoots.
- With age – and when the bush is well established – each year cut out a few of the older shoots to make way for younger ones.
- Then cut back the remaining branches to half of their length. This will encourage the development of fresh shoots.

Another pruning method is to treat them in the same way as hybrid tea roses This is especially suited to the shorter, bushier varieties. This method has the advantage of encouraging the development of finer flowers, but the plant's stance will not be so attractive. Nevertheless, it is an ideal method for the small, less vigorous varieties.

ROSE HEDGES

Like other deciduous shrubs, many roses can also be formed into hedges. Their range is wide and includes floribundas, hybrid musks, many recurrent-flowering shrub roses, bourbons, gallicas and hybrid rugosas. Initially, prune plants hard to encourage shoots from their bases – this may later need to be repeated if plants produce growth too high up. Otherwise, the aim of pruning is to create an informal outline. For floribunda types, use the method on pages 36 and 37, and recurrent types on page 39.

Rosa rugosa *'Roseraie de l'Hay*

RAMBLER ROSES

RAMBLER and climbing roses are frequently thought to be the same, but they differ dramatically and the methods of pruning them are also different.

Ramblers develop long, pliable shoots during one year, which in the following season produce clusters of flowers, mainly during mid-summer.

PRUNING TECHNIQUE

• In autumn, cut out all dead and diseased wood.

• Also, sever at the plant's base all shoots that produced flowers during the current year. This will encourage the development of fresh shoots. Tie in young shoots to replace them.

• If there are insufficient young shoots (produced during the same season) to replace those that are cut out at the plant's base, leave a few of the old ones and and cut their lateral shoots back two or three buds from their bases. During the following season, cut these very old shoots out at the plant's base.

• A few varieties need only light pruning: besides cutting out their dead wood, tip back lateral shoots that have flowered. Examples of these types of varieties include 'Emily Gray' and 'Felicite et Perpetue'.

• Prune neglected ramblers by cutting out all old wood to the plant's base, even if this means that most of the shoots are removed. During the following season, it then will be easier to differentiate between old and current shoots.

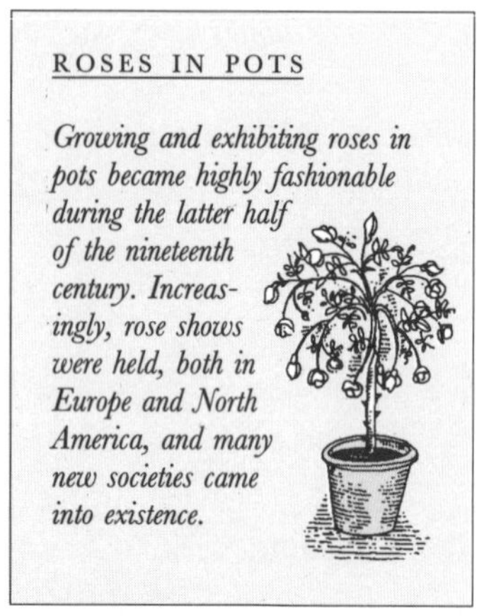

ROSES IN POTS

Growing and exhibiting roses in pots became highly fashionable during the latter half of the nineteenth century. Increasingly, rose shows were held, both in Europe and North America, and many new societies came into existence.

RAMBLERS *are usually vigorous, producing long stems each year and therefore well able to cover arches and trellises. 'Albertine' is well-known climber, as well as 'Sanders' White' which is a Wichuraiana type with small, semi-double, deliciously-fragrant flowers.*

CLIMBING ROSES

THESE are the traditional roses that clothe walls and create a galaxy of flowers in large clusters during the latter part of early summer and into mid-summer. Many varieties also have small flushes of flowers in autumn.

These climbers are derived from several sources: some are natural climbers, a few sports of bush hybrid tea or floribunda varieties, while others have more complex ancestry.

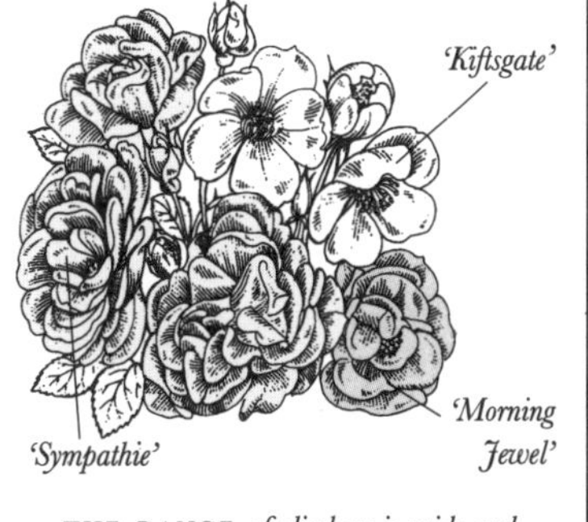

THE RANGE *of climbers is wide and includes varieties developed from naturally climbing rose species such as 'Kiftsgate', a variety of* Rosa filipes, *a true climber. Others include climbing forms of floribundas, like 'Morning Jewel', while 'Sympathie' is a Kordessi climber and raised by the German Wilhelm Kordes in 1964.*

PRUNING TECHNIQUE

- In late winter or early spring, cut out all dead, thin, weak, twiggy and diseased shoots.
- Most climbers flower on shoots produced during that same year. Therefore, build up a permanent framework of branches of well-spaced branches that will be able to clothe the wall.
- Cut back short laterals which produced flowers during the previous year to two or three buds.
- If vigorous young shoots appear high up on the plant, leave them to extend the plant's framework. In autumn tie them to the supports, and in spring secure them properly and cut off only damaged or soft tips.

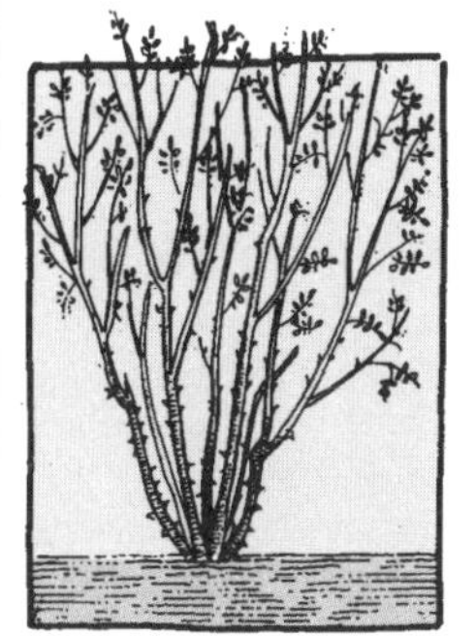

1. CLIMBING *roses have stiffer stems than ramblers, as well as a more permanent framework of branches. For this reason, build up a strong framework of well-spaced branches that clothe the wall.*

2. PRUNE *out twiggy, weak, dead, crossing and diseased wood in late winter or early spring. Also, cut back short laterals which produced flowers during the previous year.*

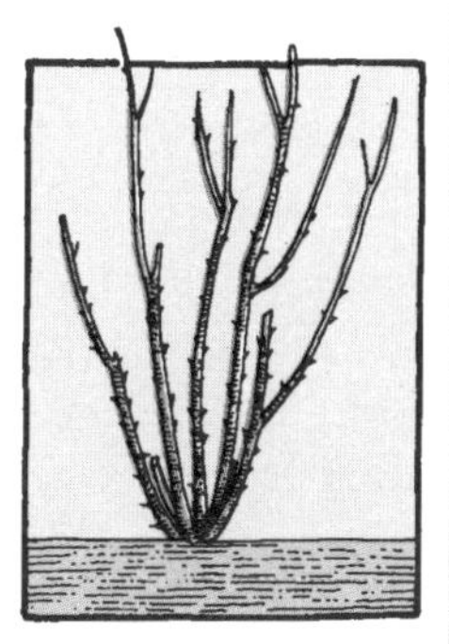

3. DURING *the previous year, strong growths will have developed. In autumn, temporarily tie them to the supporting framework. In spring, secure them properly and cut off damaged tips.*

RED AND WHITE CURRANTS

BOTH of these two soft fruits are grown on 'legs': that is, they have short stems that connect the branches to the ground. Gooseberry bushes are also grown on a leg. This is a significant difference from blackcurrants, which have a bushy base with many stems arising from the soil.

INITIAL TRAINING

When a young red or white currant bush is bought, it will have been raised from a cutting about 30cm/12in long and where all but the top three or four buds were removed. The lower 10cm/4in of the cutting would have been inserted in the ground, thereby producing a plant with a clear stem about 10cm/4in long. Thereafter, it is essential that this leg remains clear of shoots.

When bought as a young, bare-rooted plant, it will have been set in the ground at any time from late autumn to late winter. Pruning does not begin until the winter of the following year, when it has formed several branches and its roots are established.

- During the first winter after being planted, cut each shoot back by half, pruning to an outward-pointed bud. At the same time, cut out, at their bases, all crossing, weak and dead stems.
- In the winter of the second year, cut back all shoots made during the previous summer by about 20cm/8in. Also, cut all lateral shoots (those growing from the main stems) to within two buds of their bases. Additionally, remove crossing shoots so that light and air can enter the bush.
- During the third winter, cut back shoots made during the previous summer by 10–15cm/4–6in. Also, cut back all laterals to within two buds of their bases. Check that the plant's shape is even and

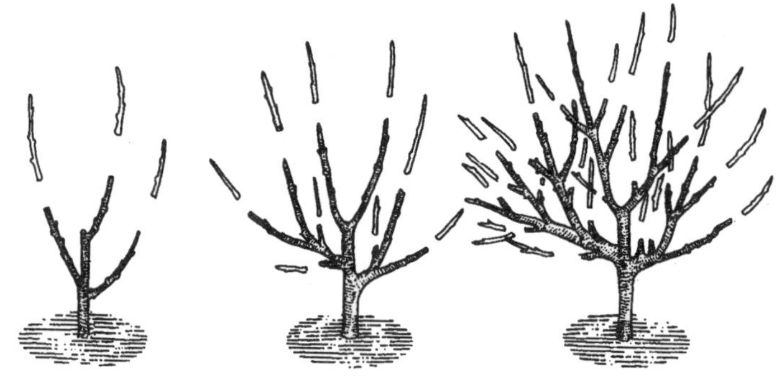

1. RED *and white currant bushes are winter pruned in the same way. During their first year after being planted, cut all shoots back by half, pruning to an outward-pointed bud. Also, completely cut out crossing, weak and dead stems.*

2. DURING *the following winter, cut back all shoots made during the previous summer by about 20cm/8in, and lateral ones (those growing from the main stems) to within two buds of their bases. Also, cut out crossing shoots.*

3. IN *the third winter, cut back all shoots made during the previous summer by 10–15cm/4–6in. Also, cut back all laterals to within two buds of their bases. Check that the plant's shape is even and not lop-sided, and remove crossing shoots.*

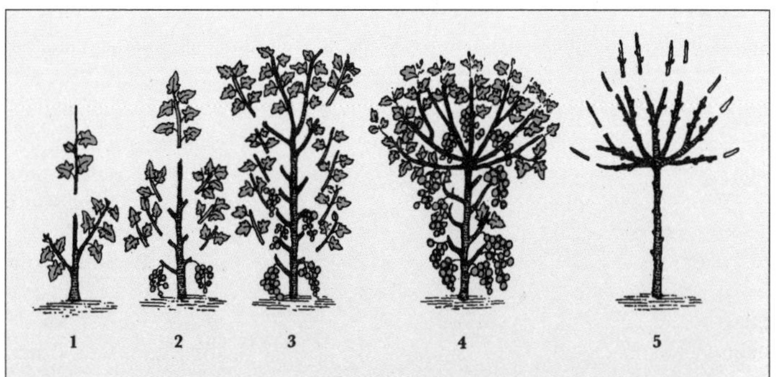

CREATING A STANDARD RED CURRANT

Standard red currants take several years to develop. They are normal red currant bushes, but on stems 75–90cm/2½–3ft high. The development of the stem, although time consuming, is easy and the only problem is to maintain growth before the head is formed.

1. DURING *the plant's first year, secure the main stem to a stout cane. Allow the main stem to grow unhindered, but cut back the lower shoots in summer to form fruiting spurs. Eventually, these will be removed.*

2. IN *the second year, allow the central stem to grow, but cut back the sideshoots to 7.5cm/3in long in summer.*

3. DURING *the third year – when the stem is about 90cm/3ft high – allow four or five shoots to develop at its top to form the head. Cut these shoots back by half in winter and prune lateral shoots to two buds long.*

4. IN *the fourth year, allow the shoots at the head to develop, cutting them back by about 15cm/6in in winter. Cut lateral shoots in the head back to within two buds of their bases. By now, the head will be well developed.*

5. DURING *the following winter, lightly trim shoots at the plant's head, cut back lateral shoots and those growing from the stem.*

not lop-sided, and remove crossing shoots that cross the plant's centre.

- In subsequent years, red and white currants produce fruit buds in clusters at the bases of one-year-old shoots and on short spurs on the older wood. A permanent framework of shoots is therefore needed, with fresh spurs being create by cutting back sideshoots.

As stems grow old, they need replacement and this is achieved by cutting a few out each year.

RED *currants are principally used for cooking, although sometimes eaten as a dessert. White currants are invariably eaten as a dessert.*

SUMMER PRUNING

As well as pruning the bushes in winter, prune them at the end of early summer. Shorten lateral shoots to about five leaves, but do not cut the leading stems. This helps to encourage the development of fruiting spurs without producing vegetative growth.

As with all highly-trained fruit bushes and trees, summer pruning is essential to encourage fruit-bud development.

BLACKCURRANTS

UNLIKE red and white currant bushes that grow on short legs, blackcurrants create a mass of stems from ground level. Therefore, they must be pruned to encourage new shoots from their bases.

Because blackcurrants develop many new shoots each year, as well as being pruned they must be planted in fertile soil, fed copiously and mulched in early summer. Use well-decomposed compost or manure to support the amount of growth the plant has to make.

BLACKCURRANTS *are superb in pies, tarts, jams and jellies.*

Immediately after planting, cut the entire plant to less than 5cm/2in above the soil's surface.

No attempt must be made to let bushes develop fruit in their first year. Their sole energy must be devoted to developing strong, new shoots and a large root-system. During the first autumn after being planted, cut down the weakest shoots that formed during summer. Further growths will develop during the following season and will become fruiting shoots.

INITIAL TRAINING

During its dormant period, from late autumn to early spring, select a well-rooted bush and plant it fractionally deeper than before to allow for settlement of loose soil around the roots. The soil-mark on the stem indicates the earlier planting depth.

SECOND AND SUBSEQUENT YEARS

In autumn, after fruits have been picked, cut back to their bases all shoots that produced fruits during the previous summer. This will leave the fresh, new shoots that formed during summer to bear fruits in the following year.

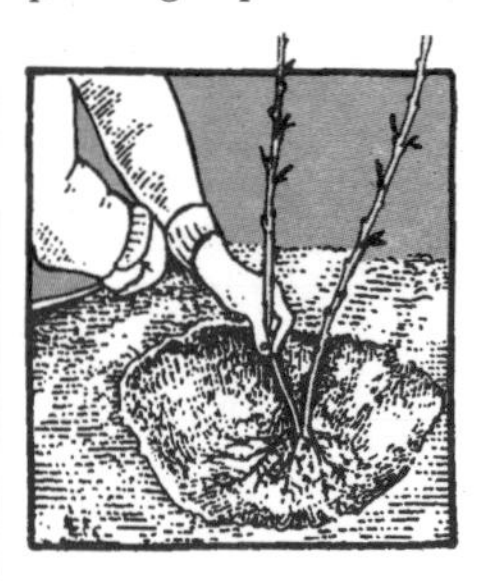

1. PLANT *bare-rooted blackcurrant bushes from late autumn to early spring. Dig out a hole large enough to accommodate the roots. Set the plant slightly deeper than before to allow for settlement of the soil.*

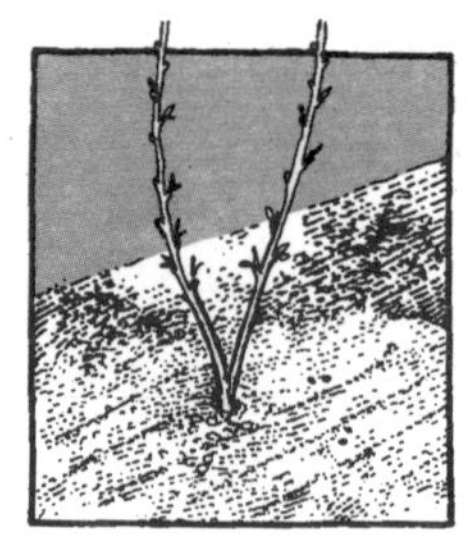

2. SPREAD *out the roots and work fine soil around them, covering and firming it in layers rather than all at one time. Lightly rake the surface to remove depressions and foot prints in which rain would settle.*

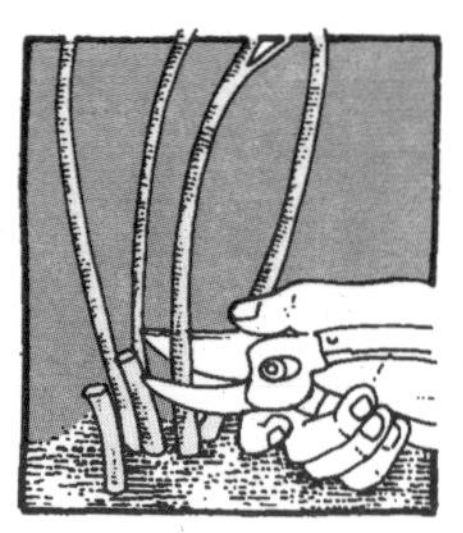

3. IMMEDIATELY *after planting, cut down all stems to within 5cm/2in of the soil's surface. This is essential, as no attempt should be made to produce fruit during the first season after planting.*

GOOSEBERRIES

LIKE red and white currants, gooseberry bushes are grown on short stems, descriptively known as 'legs'.

Plant young, bare-rooted gooseberry bushes in winter. During summer they develop shoots which in the following winter are pruned back by half to two-thirds. Sever them just above an upward-pointing bud.

Additionally, cut lateral shoots 5–7.5cm/2–3in long. Completely remove crossing and damaged shoots to ensure both light and air penetrates to the centre.

GOOSEBERRIES *are ideal for eating fresh, stewing and making into pies.*

As well as pruning in winter, at the end of early summer shorten all lateral shoots to about five leaves to encourage the formation of fruit buds. Pruning at this time does not encourage masses of growth. If shoots appear on the plant's stem, remove them immediately as it must be kept clear. Cut them off with secateurs close to their bases – do not leave short, unsightly snags.

FOLLOWING YEAR

In winter cut back, by one-third to a half, all shoots produced during the previous summer. Also, cut back laterals and completely remove crossing shoots.

In later years, cut back by a third all shoots produced during the previous summer and continue to cut back laterals. Occasionally, it is necessary to cut out whole shoots if the plant's centre becomes congested.

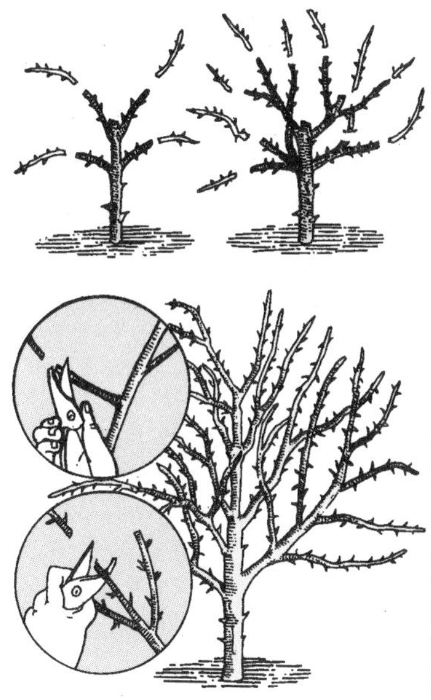

YOUNG, *newly planted gooseberry bushes (top) are initially pruned severely in winter by cutting back shoots by half to two-thirds. Later, winter pruning is less severe. Established bushes (above) have their main shoots cut by a third. Additionally, cut back laterals to 5–7.5cm/2–3in.*

EXHIBITION GOOSEBERRIES

Produce large gooseberries by:
- *Regularly syringing the bushes throughout summer*
- *Mulching the soil in summer to prevent moisture loss, keep the soil cool and to feed the plants*
- *Feed copiously in summer*
- *Thinning out to leave the shapliest and best berries*

RASPBERRIES

FEW summer fruits are as succulent and tasty as newly-picked raspberries. They are borne on long stems known as canes that develop from soil-level and, collectively with blackberries and hybrid berries, are known as cane fruits.

Most raspberries bear fruits in mid-summer on canes produced during the previous year, and these are known as summer-fruiting types. There are also varieties that develop fruits from late summer into autumn. These are widely known as autumn-fruiting raspberries and bear fruits on shoots developed during the same year. Therefore, there is a distinct difference in the way and time autumn-fruiting types are pruned – detailed on the opposite page.

RASPBERRIES *are a popular summer fruit, usually eaten fresh although some are made into jam.*

PLANTING

Both summer and autumn-fruiting raspberries are best planted in late autumn or early winter, although in cold areas this can continue to early spring. Prepare the soil by adding generous amounts of compost and manure, then dig out a deep trench for the roots.

Space the canes 38–45cm/15–18in apart in rows with about 1.5m/5ft between them. Orientate the canes north to south to ensure even growth on both sides of the row. Immediately after pruning, cut the canes of both varieties to 30cm/12in high.

If planted in winter, summer-fruiting types will bear fruits eighteen months later; autumn types in late summer and autumn of the same year.

1. PLANT *young raspberry canes in autumn or early winter, although it can be undertaken up to early spring. Dig out a trench, deep and wide enough to accommodate the roots. If possible, orientate the rows north to south.*

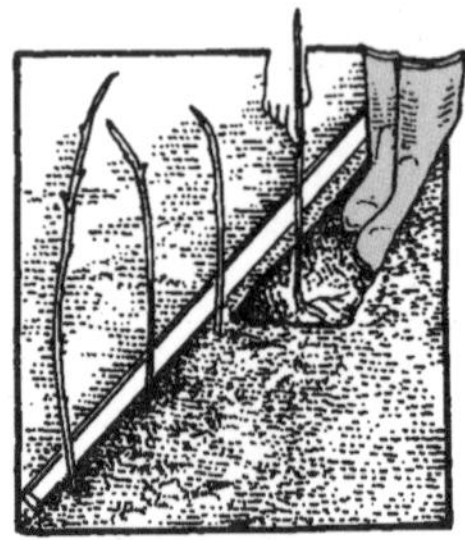

2. PLANT *the canes 38–45cm/15–18in apart in rows with about 1.5m/5ft between them. Ensure that the roots are well spread out and planted slightly deeper than before. The old soil-mark can usually be seen on the cane.*

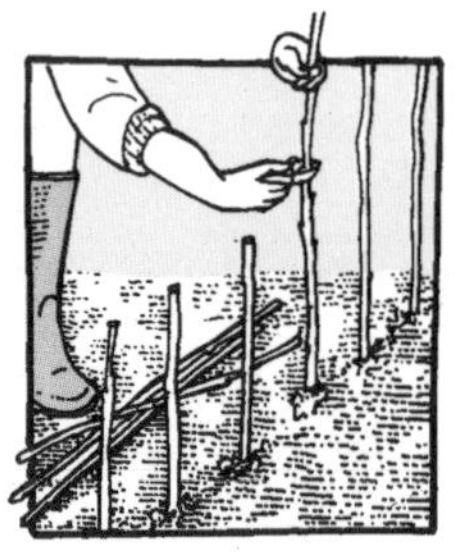

3. FIRM *soil around the roots and cut the canes of both summer and autumn-fruiting varieties to 30cm/12in above the surface. This prevents them fruiting too soon and encourages the development of strong root-systems.*

1. PRUNE *established summer-fruiting raspberries in autumn. Cut out at their bases all old stems that produced fruit during summer. Leave the young shoots unpruned.*

2. AS *the young stems grow, space them out and tie to the supporting wires. Secure them individually or with a long piece of string looped around the canes and then the wires.*

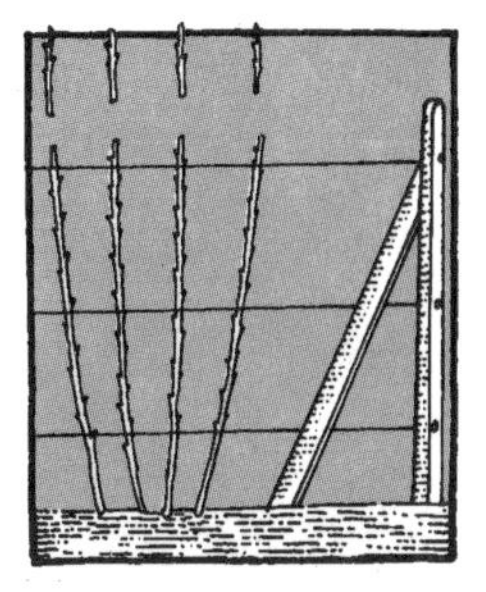

3. IN *late winter, cut back the tips of the canes to just above the top supporting wire. This concentrates growth on the lower buds and subsequently improves the quality of fruits.*

ESTABLISHED PLANTS

Prune established summer-fruiting varieties in autumn. Because these develop canes one year that bear fruits during the following one, regularly cut out to their bases all canes that have produced fruits. Young canes are then spaced out, tied to their supports and allowed to develop.

These young canes are usually tied individually to the supporting wires. Alternatively, loop a long piece of string along the row, taking it around the canes and then the supporting wire. The latter method holds the canes securely, but by tying them individually late-developing canes can be easily accomodated and secured.

In late winter, cut off the tips of the canes to just above the top supporting wire. This encourages the development of buds and improves fruit quality.

VARIETIES TO LOOK FOR

Summer-fruiting:
- 'Delight' – heavy crops of large fruits. Ideal for freezing.
- 'Glen Cova' – early fruiting, with flavoursome fruits.
- 'Malling Jewel' – well-known, virus resistant variety.

Autumn-fruiting:
- 'Heritage' – ideal in mild areas, with plenty of medium-sized fruits.
- 'Fallgold' – late, yellow-fruiting variety, which has sweet, medium-sized fruits.

AUTUMN-FRUITING RASPBERRIES

These develop fruits on shoots formed during the current season. Therefore, they are easier to prune than summer-fruiting varieties. During late winter, cut all canes to within 5cm/2in of the ground. This encourages the development of fresh canes that will bear fruits during the following late summer and autumn.

BLACKBERRIES AND HYBRID BERRIES

THESE succulently berried fruits require strong supports, which although costly and time-consuming to erect last for many years.

The juicy fruits ripen in mid and late summer and are borne on long shoots, known as canes, that initially developed during the previous year. Therefore, the technique of pruning these fruits is to cut out in late summer or autumn all shoots after they have borne fruits and to retain young canes. These will bear fruits during the following season.

SUPPORTS

These are essential and provided by straining four strands of 10-gauge galvanized wire between strong posts. Position the wires 90cm/3ft, 1.2m/4ft, 1.5m/5ft and 1.8m/6ft above the ground.

Fertile, moisture-retentive soil is essential and therefore before planting new canes dig in plenty of well-decayed compost or manure into the soil. Plant new canes 1.8–3m/6–10ft apart any time from autumn to spring, whenever the soil is not frozen or waterlogged. Immediately, cut them down to 25–30cm/10–12in high. This encourages the development of young, strong canes. Do not prune small, young shoots that cluster around the bases of plants: these later bear fruit.

ESTABLISHED PLANTS

Once establised, each year these plants will have two types of shoots: the ones that will produce fruits in mid- and late summer, and young ones that will bear fruits during the following year.

Therefore, the art of pruning is to cut out all shoots to their bases immediately after bearing fruits;

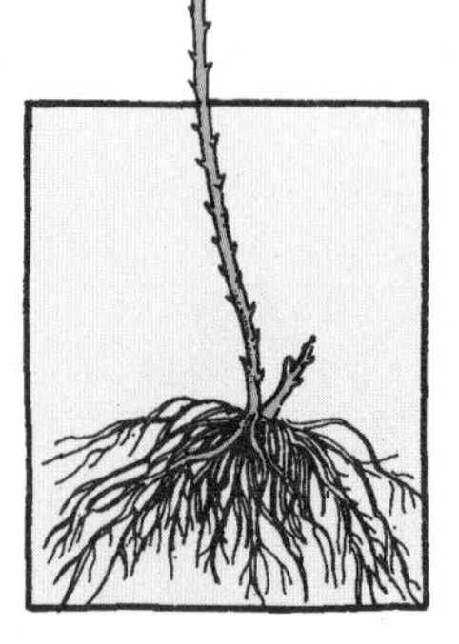

1. PLANT *young, bare-rooted blackberry and hybrid berry canes at any time between autumn and early spring, whenever the soil is not frozen or water-logged. Container-grown plants are planted when the weather allows.*

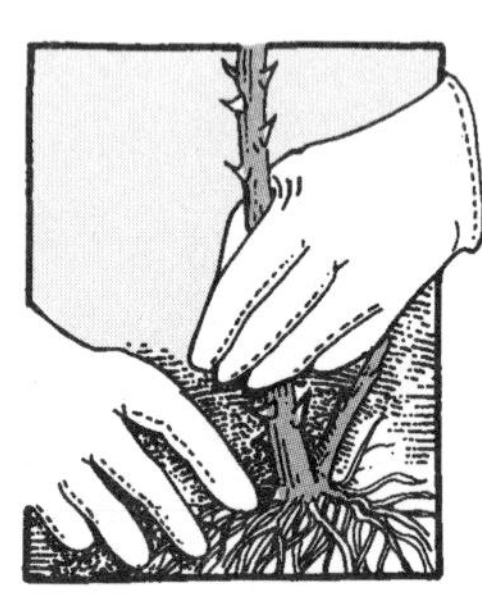

2. DIG *in plenty of organic material. Set the plants 1.8-3m/6-10ft apart and support with four wires strained between strong posts. Ensure the roots are well spread out, with friable soil firmed over them. Water them thoroughly.*

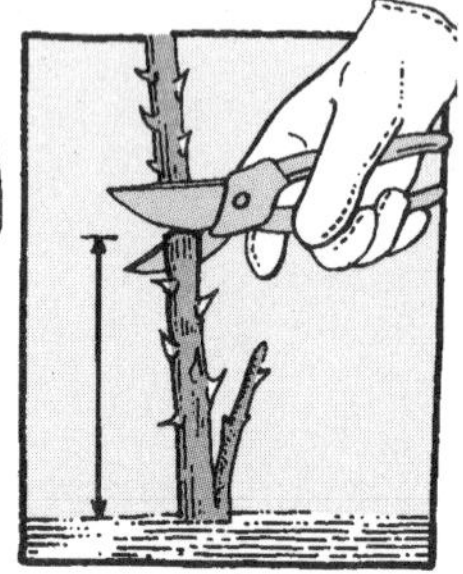

3. IMMEDIATELY *they are planted, cut back all stems to 25–30cm/10–12in above the ground. This encourages the development of shoots that later will bear fruits. Do not prune young shoots. Use gloves, as the shoots are very thorny.*

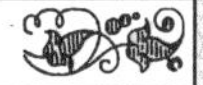

1. BLACKBERRIES *and hybrid berries develop fruits on shoots produced during the previous year. Therefore, immediately after fruiting, cut out to their bases all canes that produced fruits.*

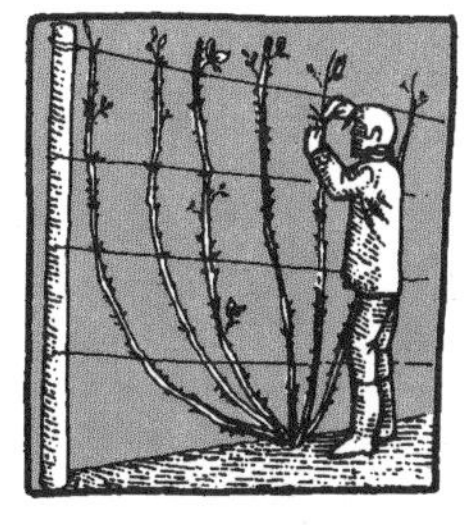

2. AFTER *pruning, spread out and tie in the young shoots that will produce fruit during the following season. Space out the shoots equally and loosely but firmly secure them to the wires.*

3. TO *encourage fresh canes, mulch the plants with well-decomposed compost or manure. At the end of winter, cut back dead cane tips to the first live and healthy bud.*

and to train and tie in young shoots so that they are all equally exposed to light and air. Additionally, in late winter – after they may have been damaged by continuous and exceptionally severe frosts – cut back all shoots tips to healthy, live buds.

LOGANBERRIES

These large-berried fruits are said to have come from North America, where Judge J. H. Logan of Santa Cruz, California, is held to have spotted a chance cross between a blackberry and raspberry more than a century ago.

Loganberries are now widely known and grown as scrambling, summer-fruiting plants.

They have a similar nature to blackberries: immediately after fruiting, cut out old canes to within 5cm/2in of the ground. The young shoots are then loosely but securely tied to supports.

Keep the two types of shoots separate: train the older ones to one side, younger ones to the other. This makes pruning slightly easier as it is then quite clear which are the ones to be cut to ground level.

PRUNING BLUEBERRIES

These well-known fruits are popular in pies and tarts. Blueberries bear fruits on the tips of the previous season's shoots. It is necessary each spring to cut out a few old shoots, as well as dead, weak and crossing ones.

In the plant's first year after being planted, prevent it developing fruits by using a finger to rub off plump fruit buds, leaving only the smaller buds that will produce leaves.

During the third year – and in all subsequent ones – prune blueberries in late winter or spring. Cut back a few of the older shoots at their bases. This initiates the formation of shoots that later will develop fruits.

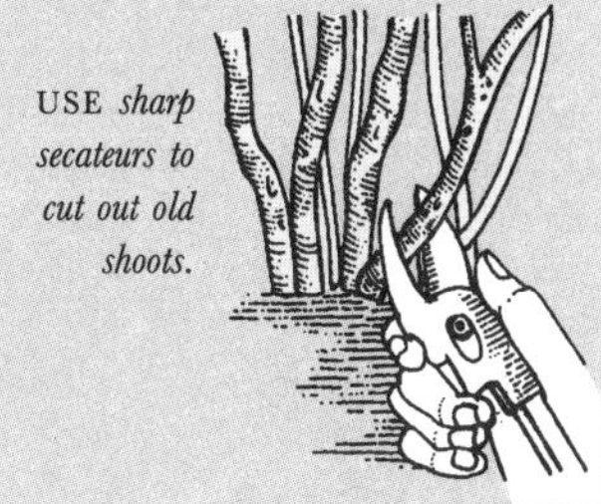

USE *sharp secateurs to cut out old shoots.*

APPLE AND PEAR BUSHES

Regular pruning is essential, initially to form a framework of branches and the desired shape; later to ensure a balance between fruit production and new growth. The initial pruning is performed in winter, when trees are in a dormant state.

APPLES *and pears are the most popular tree fruits in temperate climates.*

Most apple trees are bought either as bare-rooted trees during winter, or established and growing in containers.

Bare-rooted types are planted during winter, whenever the weather and soil allows, while container-grown types can be set in the ground at any time of year when it is not frozen or waterlogged, but avoid periods when the soil is very dry or the weather excessively hot.

YOUNG TREES

After planting a maiden tree (one that is one year old and has not produced sideshoots) cut back to about half its height during late winter.

Cut just above a bud. This causes the maiden tree to extend its growth upwards during the following summer, as well as to develop sideshoots.

During the following winter, reduce the lengths of all shoots by half, at the same time removing dead, crossing and damaged shoots. Ensure the tree's centre is open and free from branches.

In the following winter, prune the shoots less severely: cut main shoots by one-third. Weak, less-vigorous shoots are pruned by half to encourage stronger growth.

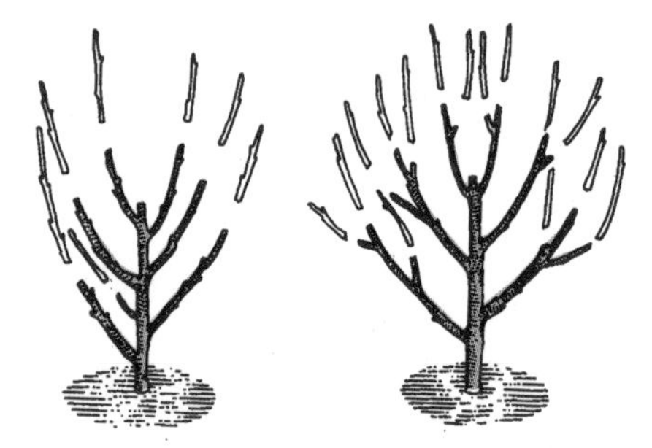

1. MOST *apple trees are bought as established bushes with several shoots forming the tree's framework. However, when planting a maiden tree, cut it to about half its height in winter, severing the stem just above a strong, healthy bud.*

2. DURING *the following summer shoots develop, and in winter are reduced by about half their lengths. Cut to outward-pointing buds. At the same time, remove dead, crossing and damage shoots, close to their bases. Always use sharp secateurs.*

3. BY *the following winter, the tree will have developed a strong framework. Cut back vigorous shoots by one-third; weak ones by a half. Select the best positioned shoots to form the permanent framework. Inspect the tree from several angles.*

PRUNING PEARS

Pears need similar pruning to apples but can, if necessary and when established, be pruned slightly more severely.

Most pears bear fruits on spurs. With these, shorten new growth formed by leading shoots by about a third and cut back laterals to three or four buds. Also, cut out overcrowded spurs and ensure the plant's centre is kept open. A few varieties – 'Josephine de Malines' and 'Jargonelle' – are tip-bearing and need only the longest laterals cut to four buds long.

SOME *apple varieties, such as Cox's Orange Pippin, bear fruits on spurs arising from their branches. Prune them to encourage the development of fresh, young spurs (see above).*

OTHER *varieties, like Worcester Pearmain, bear fruits towards the tips of shoots. Therefore, instead of cutting back shoots to encourage the development of spurs, most are left to encourage fruits to develop towards their tips (see above).*

Always make pruning cuts slightly above a bud that faces outwards.

ESTABLISHED BUSHES

Pruning established bushes uses one of two different methods, depending on the variety. Some apple varieties bear fruits on two-year-old shoots and short shoots known as spurs growing on older wood. Other varieties develop fruits on the tips of shoots formed during the previous year. A few varieties combine these two methods of fruiting.

SPUR-BEARING

During a tree's formative years, continue to cut back the tips of leading branches by about a quarter. Also, cut back young laterals that are growing too close to the leading shoots.

On older trees – apart from removing dead, overcrowded and crossing shoots – encourage the development of spurs on shoots away from the branch leaders by cutting them to about six buds long. In the following year, other shoots further up the branch can be pruned in the same way. Additionally, new shoots growing from cut-back ones are pruned to three buds each.

TIP-BEARING

These varieties bear fruits towards the tips of shoots. Prune established bushes in winter, removing crowded branches and cutting out crossing and crowded ones. At the same time prune the branch leaders: cut back the growth made during the previous year by about a third.

At the same time, leave all but the most vigorous lateral shoots unpruned. However, to encourage the development of more shoots, cut back by half those that are more than 25cm/10in long.

ESPALIER APPLES AND PEARS

TRAINED fruit trees, such as espaliers and cordons, are frequently much easier to fit into small gardens than bush types. They can be planted and trained against warm walls or alongside tiered wires tensioned between posts. Espaliers can even be formed into arches covering paths.

GETTING STARTED

Novice fruit growers may wish to start training an espalier by planting a partly-trained tree, perhaps with two or three tiers of branches. A less expensive beginning is to plant a one-year-old specimen.

The first task is to erect tiers of 10-gauge galvanized wires, the lowest one 38cm/15in above the soil and then spaced 25–30cm/10–12in apart. Allow for five or six tiers of wires.

Plant a young, bare-rooted tree in winter and cut it slightly above a bud, 5cm/2in above the lowest wire. During summer, when growth begins, rub out all buds except the top one and a couple on either side that will form two arms. Select buds that face the intended direction of growth. Insert a cane to support the leading shoot. Also, use two 1.2m/4ft canes to support the two 'arms'. Initially, train them at 45 degree angles: if one grows faster, raise the angle of the other one to encourage more rapid growth and to make them even.

This is based on the fact that vertical shoots always grow faster than horizontal ones, although the latter will produce fruits earlier than those that are upright. Towards the end of the growing season, lower the canes and tie them to the horizontal wires.

PRUNE *a maiden tree to a bud 5cm/2in above the bottom wire (right). In summer it will form side branches and further growth at its top (far right). During the following winters, cut the leading shoot above the next wire until five or six tiers have been formed (below and below right).*

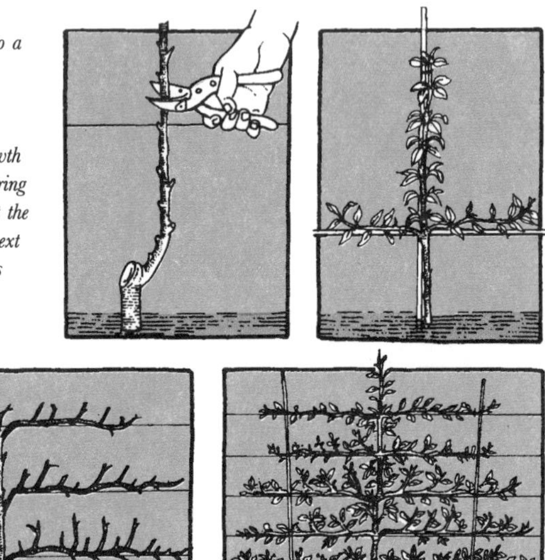

In the second winter, the central stem will have grown above the next wire. Again, cut it off 5cm/2in above the wire and remove all buds, except the top three, that are between the first and second wire.

During the second summer, train the top two shoots in the same way as in the previous year. Also, cut back to the third leaf all sideshoots growing on the bottom tier. Additionally, lightly cut back their ends to leave a short piece of new wood. It is essential not to cut into the older wood.

In the following season, repeat these treatments. When the central stem reaches the desired height, cut it off slightly above the top supporting wire.

PARTLY-TRAINED ESPALIERS

These save two or three years of work, but because they are larger it takes longer for them to become established. They are also more expensive to buy.

Before planting, measure the distances between the tiers of branches and then erect supporting wires to suit them. If wrongly spaced, the branches cannot be supported properly

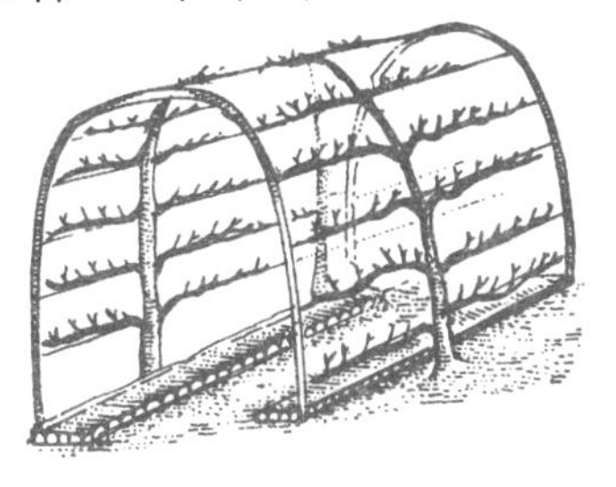

APPLE *and pear trees are occasionally trained to create arches 1.8–2.4m/6–8ft high and 2.4–3m/8–10ft wide, and are especially attractive when forming a canopy over gravel paths. They are like espaliers, with lateral stems trained on wires.*

CORDONS

Cordon apples and pears can be grown in rows alongside paths and trained between 35 and 45 degree angles up wires tensioned between posts. Instead of tying cordon stems directly to the wires, first secure them to strong bamboo canes. In mid- to late summer, cut back lateral shoots (right) to the third leaf above the basal cluster. Also, cut back the end of the main shoot (left) to leave a short length of new wood.

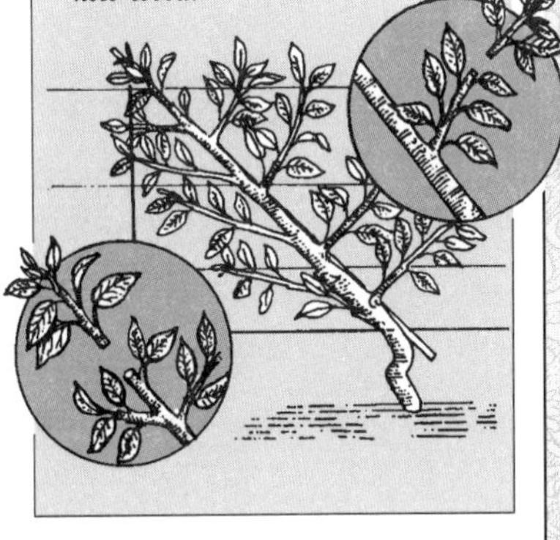

Plant bare-rooted plants during their dormant period in winter and when the soil is not frozen or waterlogged. Container-grown trees are planted at any time, whenever the weather and soil allows – but not during droughts when the soil is very dry.

Spread out the roots and firm soil in layers around them. At this stage, only loosely tie the main stem and tiers to the wires. It is possible that the soil will settle slightly, and unless the branches are intially tied loosely they may be put under unnecessary tension.

After a couple of months, check the tree and secure the ties properly. Also, check the ties regularly to ensure they have not perished and are too loose.

PLUMS AND GAGES

Stone fruits, such as plums and gages, are succulent and juicy. Dessert varieties need a sunnier and more sheltered position than cooking varieties, which tolerate greater exposure to low temperatures. They are sometimes grown as fan-trained trees against warm walls, but are usually planted as half-standards, with an eventual trunk length of 1–1.2m/3½–4ft. Alternatively, they are grown as bushes, with a 60–75cm/2–2½ft clear stem that forms a trunk.

PLUMS *and gages are succulent fruits, eaten fresh, bottled or made into jam.*

HALF-STANDARDS

Plums and gages are susceptible to silver leaf disease if they are pruned in autumn or winter when dormant. Therefore, always prune them in spring when growth is beginning and wounds will heal over quickly.

Training and pruning a one-year-old (maiden) tree as a half-standard is not difficult, although it takes four or five years before the tree's main framework is formed. Buying a partly-trained tree clearly reduces this period.

Plant a bare-rooted maiden tree in winter. At this stage it will be about 1.5m/5ft high with thin shoots growing from its stem.

Support the tree, either by inserting a vertical stake while the tree is being planted, or by an H-shaped one afterwards. Inserting a

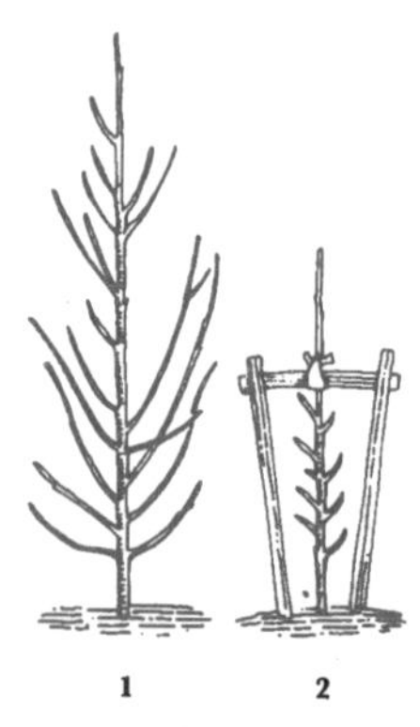

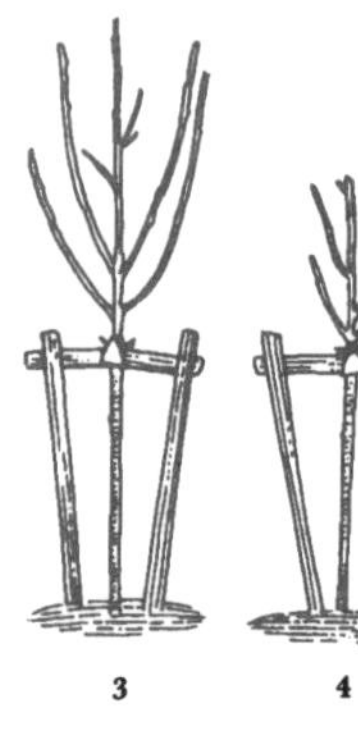

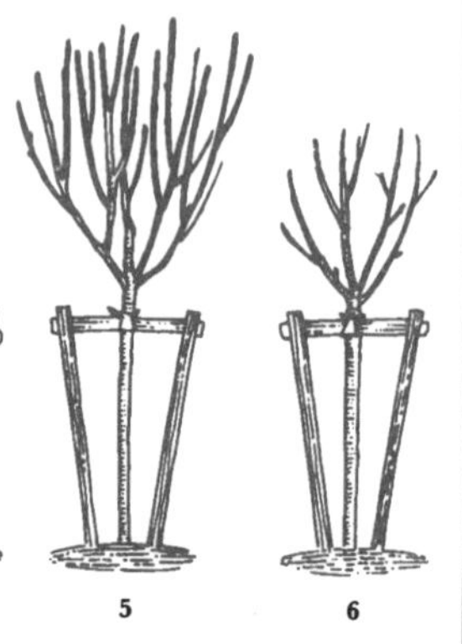

PLANT *a bare-rooted, maiden plum tree in winter* (**1**). *Support the stem with a vertical stake or H-formation* (**2**). *Cut back the main stem to 1.3m/4½ft, about 15–20cm/6–8in above the stake. Cut back side-shoots to 10cm/4in long.*

A TWO-*year-old plum tree during the following winter* (**3**). *It will have developed long shoots from its top. Prune these just before growth begins in spring, cutting them back by half* (**4**). *These will form the main branches later.*

DURING *the following summer the head will develop further stems, which are cut back by half in spring. By the following winter, these will have formed a large head* (**5**), *which in spring are again reduced by half* (**6**).

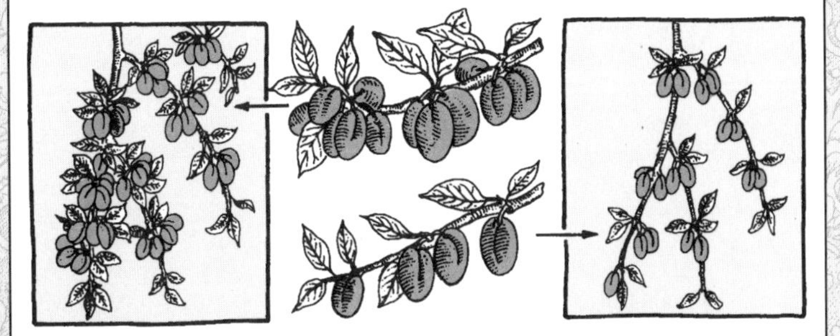

THINNING *is essential when plum trees are carrying a heavy crop of fruits. If unthinned (left), the fruits remain small, flavourless and poorly coloured. Also, branches bearing excessive amounts of fruit may break off the tree. Thinning fruits is carried out in two stages: first, when the fruits are the size of hazelnuts and when the stones have formed, usually in early summer. The second thinning is when fruits are about twice that size, leaving 5cm/2in between them.*

vertical one after planting may damage the roots. The top bar of the H-stake should be 1–1.2m/ 3½–4ft high. In spring, cut the top of the plant's stem to 1.3m/ 4½ft high, about 15–20cm/6–8in above the stake. Also, cut back all sideshoots to 10cm/4in long. These are later removed, but initially are left to assist the main stem to thicken.

During the following summer, shoots develop from its top. In spring, cut these back by half. Also, cut out all crossing, rubbing, thin and dead shoots. At this stage, try to form a framework of evenly spaced branches.

In the following summer, further shoots will develop, and in spring are cut back by half, at the same time removing crossing and thin shoots. Also, cut off the twiggy shoots growing from the stem.

Repeat this process during the following spring, by which time the tree will be four years old and have a good framework of branches. In subsequent years, cut the shoots less severely, removing only one-third of their new growth and removing congested and crossing shoots.

FAN-TRAINED PLUMS

A warm, sunny wall is an ideal place to grow a fan-trained plum or gage tree. Such places produce the sweetest-flavoured gages. Established trees are available with several stems branching in a fan from their bases. It is, however, possible to start with a one-year-old tree. Each fan-trained tree needs 4.5–5.4m/ 15–18ft of wall space, with the plant positioned 15–23cm/ 6–9in from the wall. Its pruning is the same as for peaches *(see pages 56 and 57)**.*

A mature fan-trained gage will produce 7–11kg/15–25lb of fruit.

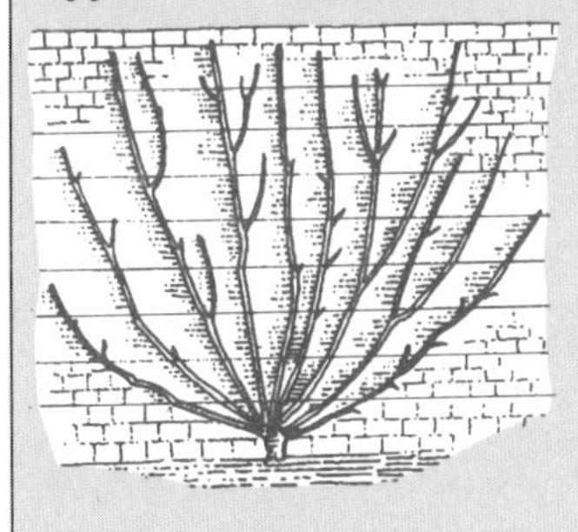

PEACHES AND NECTARINES

Most peaches and nectarines are grown on fan-trained trees against warm, sunny walls. The aim is to train the tree to fill the wall with branches that radiate from near the main stem's base. They will then receive the maximum amount of light and air, as well as benefiting from warmth radiated by the wall. Growing and training peaches and nectarines in this way is not quick and it will take several years to form the fan. Plum and gage trees are also often grown as fans, in the same way.

PEACHES *and nectarines are delicious, juicy fruits. Peaches have a fuzzy covering, whereas nectarines are smooth skinned.*

MAIDEN TREE

Plant a bare-rooted, one-year-old (maiden) tree in winter, about 15cm/6in from the base of a warm, sunny wall. In spring, cut the main stem to about 60cm/2ft high and just above a bud. Remove side shoots, or buds – all but the top five. Although only three good buds are needed (the top one to produce vertical growth and the two laterals) leave a couple more in case the others are damaged. They can be removed later.

During the following summer, the bud at the top will continue growth upwards, while two shoots – one at each side – are encouraged to form the branches. When it can be seen that they are growing strongly, remove the others.

Insert canes to enable the vertical and lateral shoots to be supported. In spring, sever the vertical shoot fractionally above the two sideshoots, and cut back the side branches to buds on their upper sides and 38–45cm/15–18in from the main stem.

During the following summer, encourage shoots to develop from

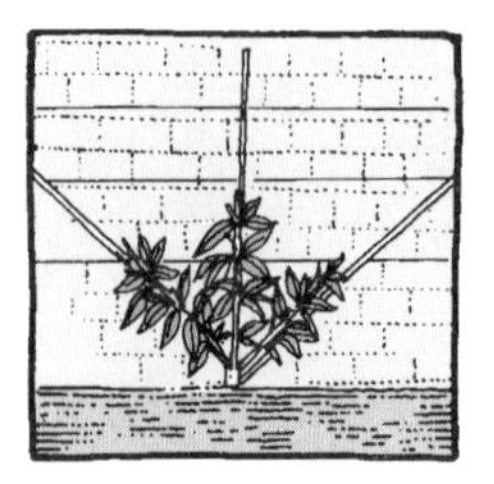

1. IT IS *possible to start with a one-year-old fan-trained tree, but to save time, two- or three-year-old ones can be bought. The two-year-old plant shown above has developed two strong sideshoots, as well as terminal growth.*

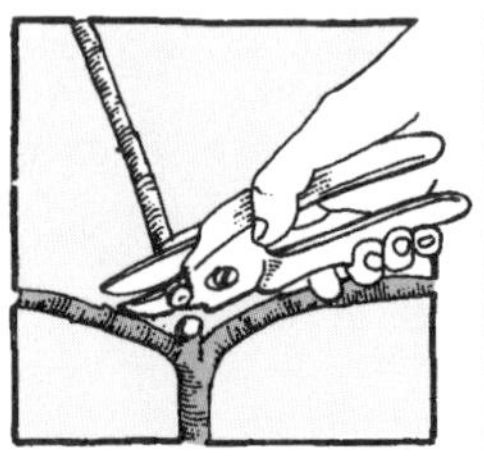

2. IN SPRING, *when new growth begins, cut off the terminal stem to just above the sideshoots, taking care not to damage them. This pruning directs growth into shoots that subsequently will develop into the lowest branches on the fan.*

3. AS WELL *as severing the leading shoot, also cut sideshoots to buds on their upper sides, 38–45cm/15–18in from the main stem. In summer, allow them to grow, and select two young shoots on the upper side and one the under side to develop.*

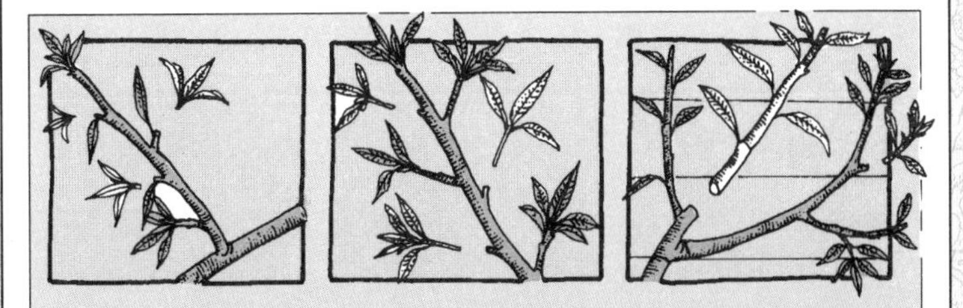

PRUNING ESTABLISHED FAN-SHAPED TREES

1. PRUNE *established fan trees in spring and summer. In spring, prune one-year-old shoots. Leave a replacement shoot at the base of each one, but reduce other growths to a single leaf.*

2. BRANCHES *that have been trained and tied in as extensions to the main framework are also pruned in spring. Shoots growing from it are carefully thinned to about 15cm/6in apart, preventing congestion later.*

3. AFTER *the fruits have been picked, prune lateral shoots that carried the crop back to the replacement shoots that were left at their bases. These are the ones that appeared in the first illustration.*

these two arms. On each side, allow two buds on the upper side and one on the lower side to produce shoots. Tie these to canes and then to a framework of wires.

By the following spring they will have developed into long shoots. Cut each shoot back to a triple bud so that 45–60cm/1½–2ft of ripened wood remains on each fan. In the following year, allow further shoots on the insides of the inner branches to develop.

FOLLOWING SUMMER

During the following summer, allow each of the eight branches to grow, tying new shoots first on to canes and then on the wires. Also, rub out all buds growing directly towards or away from the wall to keep the shape flatter.

Allow shoots to develop every 15cm/6in apart on the tops and bottoms of the branches. Carefully rub out those shoots that are not wanted as the fan develops.

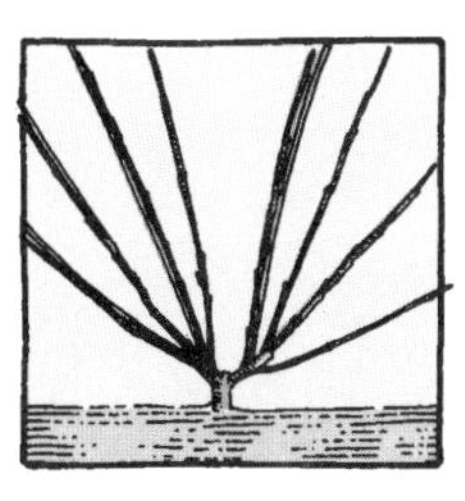

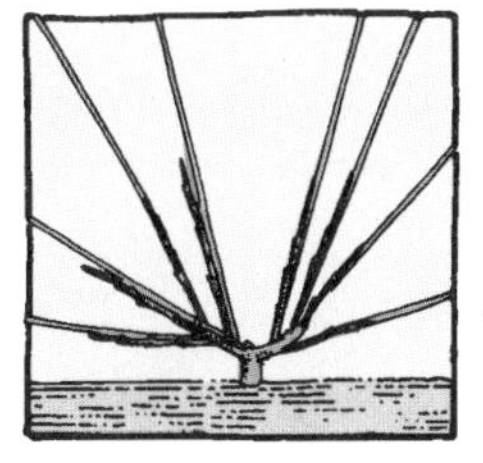

4. IN THE *following summer, shoots will develop from the lowest branches and start to fill in the fan's centre. Each shoot is tied to a strong cane, which is then secured to a tiered framework or wires spaced 20–25cm/ 8–10in apart.*

5. IN WINTER, *ensure the canes – together with the shoots tied to them – are spaced equally apart, but leaving the centre of the fan open for the development of further shoots. The centre is always the last part of the fan to fill with shoots.*

6. DURING *spring, cut back each branch to a triple bud so that 45–60cm/ 1½–2ft of ripened wood remains on each fan. In the following summer, shoots on the inner sides of the two central branches are allowed to develop.*

OUTDOOR GRAPES AND FIGS

GRAPES are frequently grown in greenhouses in cool climates, but in warm countries are cultivated outdoors. Even in temperate climates, it is increasingly possible to grow outdoor grapes through the introduction of hardier varieties.

The method of pruning greenhouse and outdoor grape-vines is basically the same, and the objective is to grow a single rod (plant stem) and to encourage the development of sideshoots which eventually will develop into strong branches and bear fruits. To ensure the branches are spaced out, train them on alternative sides of the rod.

Incidentally, pruning commercially grown outdoor grapes is more complicated than the method suggested here, which is best suited to home gardeners.

OUTDOOR GRAPES

Tiers of horizontal, 10-gauge galvanized wires spaced 30cm/12in apart and 13–15cm/5–6in from a wall are essential. Position the bottom wire about 45cm/1½ft above the ground and choose a sheltered, warm and sunny wall.

Plant bare-rooted and container-grown vines in spring, then shorten the main shoot (rod) to about 60cm/2ft high. Cut off all other shoots to a single bud, and tie the rod first to a cane and then to the horizontal wires.

1. DURING *the first summer, prune the lateral shoots. Pinch out – or use scissors – their ends just beyond the fifth leaf. Also, remove flowers before they develop into fruits.*

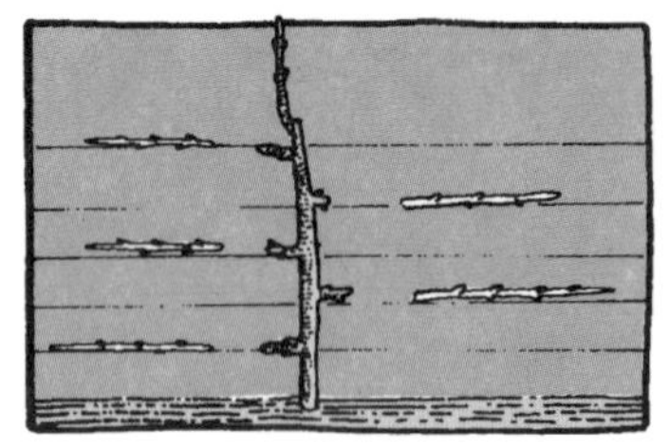

2. IN AUTUMN, *cut back the rod to half of the growth it made during the current season. Also, cut back all lateral shoots to form stubs, each with only two buds.*

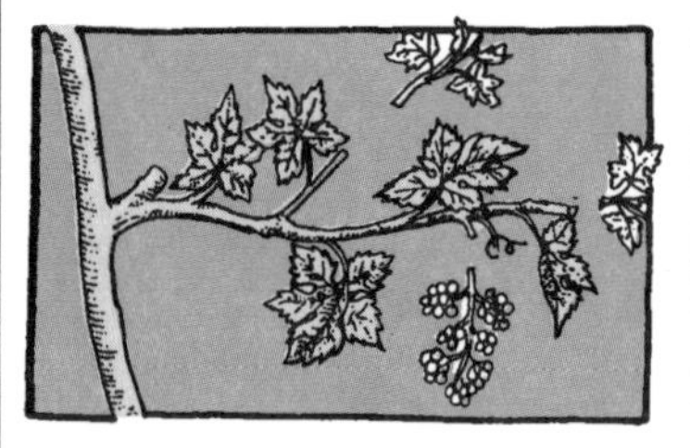

3. DURING *the following summer, cut back lateral shoots to just beyond the fifth leaf. Also, cut back sub-laterals to one leaf and remove all flowers before they develop fruits.*

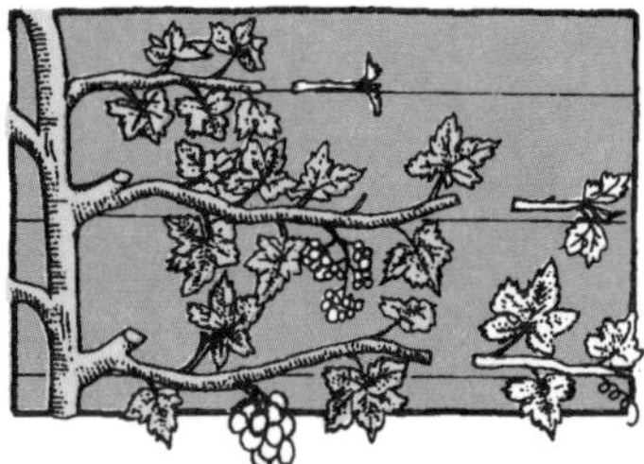

4. IN AUTUMN, *cut back laterals to leave two buds at their bases. In summer (above) allow two or three bunches to develop and prune to two leaves beyond them.*

PRUNING SEQUENCE

Pruning begins in the first summer after being planted. Either pinch back or use sharp scissors to cut lateral shoots to just beyond the fifth leaf. Also, cut off all flower trusses. If young vines are allowed to flower and then develop fruits this will weaken and delay their development.

- In the following autumn, cut back the rod to half of the growth it made during the current season. The purpose is to remove soft, unripened wood. Cut to just above a bud. Additionally, cut all lateral shoots back to leave two buds at their bases.

Vines are vigorous plants and every year they are pruned in this manner. Each spring, new shoots develop that will bear fruits.

- In the following summer, again cut back laterals to just beyond the fifth leaf. Also, sever the sub-laterals to just beyond a single leaf and remove all flowers.
- During the following autumn, again cut back the vertical, leading shoot by half, as well as cutting back the laterals to leave two firm, healthy buds.
- In early summer, when growth begins from the bases of laterals, allow only the strongest to develop. Allow two or three bunches of grapes to develop from them and prune these to two leaves beyond the young fruits.
- In autumn, again cut the rod to half of the wood made during the previous summer, as well as carefully trimming back lateral growths to two buds.
- In summer, again select the strongest shoot for each lateral. This summer, allow further laterals to develop fruits – this is a continuing process.
- When the top of the rod reaches the top wire, cut it off just above the topmost lateral.

THINNING GRAPES

THIS *is essential to ensure individual grapes are a good size. As soon as the berries start to swell, use scissors with long-pointed blades to gradually cut out the smallest berries, especially those from the bunch's centre.*

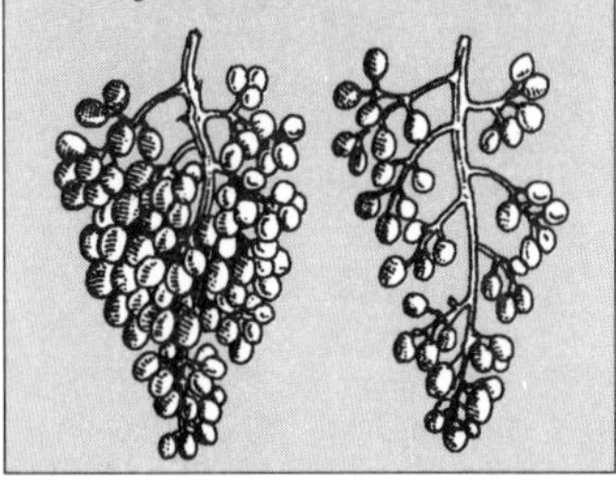

PRUNING FIGS

Figs are best grown as fans against a warm, sunny wall. Buy a two-year-old container-grown plant and specify the need for a fan-trained type. Plant it in early spring, about 15cm/6in from a wall. Instal tiered wires, 15cm/6in apart, the lowest one 45cm/1½ft above the ground and the top one 2.4m/8ft high.

In spring, cut back both branches to a bud about 45cm/1½ft from their bases. In summer, allow each branch to develop two shoots on its upper side, one on the lower side and a further one at the growing tip. As shoots develop from these, tie them first to canes, then to wires.

Once fans have been formed, trim young shoots back to five leaves in early summer.

FIGS *are succulent fruits but need a sunny and sheltered wall, and a warm climate.*

PRUNING CALENDAR

Numbers in brackets are page references.

SPRING

This is an active time for pruning plants. Here are a few reminders about some jobs.

- Prune nectarines, apricots, cherries, plums and gages in spring, when growth is beginning. In some areas, this may be in late spring (54–57)
- Prune winter-flowering shrubs as soon as the last of their flowers fade (26–27)
- Prune late summer-flowering shrubs (24–25)
- Prune *Clematis macropetala*, *C. flammula* and *C. tangutica* in mid-spring (20–21)
- Prune dogwoods *(Cornus)* in mid-spring (32)
- Prune Mop-headed Hydrangea *(Hydrangea macrophylla)* in spring (32)
- Prune callunas and summer-flowering ericas in spring (33)
- Prune roses, especially in cold regions (34–35)
- Prune climbing roses in late winter or early spring (41)
- Prune blueberries in spring (49)
- Prune the Winter-flowering Jasmine *(Jasminum nudiflorum)* after the flowers fade (20–21)
- Prune winter and spring-flowering ericas when their flowers have faded (33)
- Prune Tree Heaths in late spring (33)
- Trim back long shoots on conifers in spring (16)
- Renovate old hedges in early spring (16)
- Trim ivies in spring to restrict their growth (20–21)
- Trim back overgrown Russian Vines *(Polygonum baldschuanicum)* in spring (20–21)
- Trim daboecias in spring in cold areas (33). If pruned too early, shoots are damaged

SUMMER

This is an active time in a fruit garden: although apples and pears are regularly pruned in winter, and plums, gages, nectarines and peaches in spring when their growth begins, many benefit from summer pruning. Cutting fruit trees at this time does not encourage vigorous growth and therefore fruiting spurs can be created.

By mid-summer, early-flowering shrubs will have finished their display and can be pruned to encourage the development of shoots that will bear flowers during the following year.

- Trim hedges regularly throughout summer (14–15)
- Dead-head large-flowered rhododendrons as soon as their flowers fade (32)
- Prune spring and early summer-flowering shrubs immediately after their flowers fade (22–23)
- Cut back deciduous, newly-planted hedges formed from container-grown plants. This encourages bushiness (14–15)
- Cut out water-shoots on deciduous trees as soon as they are seen (28)
- Remove suckers from bush roses, as well as those from stems of standards (34–35)
- In late summer, cut dead flowers off Mop-head Hydrangeas *(Hydrangea macrophylla)* (32)
- Trim topiary regularly throughout summer (18–19)
- In mid-summer, summer-prune wisterias (20–21)
- Summer-prune gooseberries to encourage fruit buds (45)
- Summer-prune red and white currants (42–43)
- Summer-prune espalier, and trained fruit trees (52–57)

AUTUMN

With the advent of cold, frosty weather and falling leaves, autumn becomes a time for clearing up. In mild areas, roses can be pruned, but in cold regions it is best left until early spring. However, all bush roses (especially those in exposed, windy areas) benefit from having long stems cut back to prevent wind buffeting them and loosening their roots in the soil. This especially applies to young bushes, when perhaps their roots are not fully established.

Ensure all pruning equipment is sharp and able to create clean cuts. Also, check that ladders used for reaching high branches are sound and able to support your weight. Long-reach pruners often need the leverage mechanism oiled to ensure easy use. Check secateurs and loppers to make sure their blades have not been bent while being forced to cut too thick shoots. Spare parts are available for some secateurs.

- Prune trees with sappy wood, such as conifers, birches, Horse Chestnuts and some maples, in late autumn (8–9). If pruned in summer when their sap is rising strongly they will bleed profusely and be damaged.
- Prune daboecias in late autumn, or spring in cold regions (33).
- Prune the ever popular rambler roses in autumn (40).
- Prune summer-fruiting raspberries in autumn (46–47). Autumn-fruiting ones are left until late winter.
- Cut away the old stems of the herbaceous climber Yellow-leaved Hop in autumn (20–21).
- Prune bush roses in autumn in mild areas (34–37). In cold areas, this job is best left until warmer weather in early spring.
- Prune blackberries and hybrid berries (48–49).

WINTER

Garden hygiene is essential to prevent some fruit pests and diseases spreading as well as continuing from one season to another. After pruning fruit trees, collect up the prunings and burn them. Do not just leave them on the ground.

In areas where winters are exceptionally severe and long, delay pruning, especially with roses: too early pruning encourages the development of young shoots that are soon damage by low temperatures.

- Prune the floriferous wisteria in late winter (20–21).
- Prune climbing roses in late winter or early spring (41).
- Prune autumn-fruiting raspberries in late winter (47).
- Prune the distinctively-flowered Passion Flower *(Passiflora caerulea)* in late winter (20–21).
- Cut off the top of coniferous hedges when they reach the desired height (16).
- Prune bush roses in early winter when growing them in very mild areas (34–37).
- Cut back newly-planted, bare-rooted deciduous hedges to encourage bushy growth (14–15). If this task is neglected, the hedge will have a bare, unsightly base.
- Cut back large branches on trees during winter – but not those on cherry trees or any other members of the *Prunus* family (13).
- Cut off long stems from bush roses to reduce the amount of foliage exposed to wind. This reduces the chances of roots being loosened in the soil.
- Prune gooseberries (45).
- Winter-prune apples and pears to create the formation of a sound, strong framework of branches that will bear fruiting spurs (50–51).

USEFUL PRUNING TERMS

ANVIL SECATEUR: *Type of secateur where a cutting blade cuts against a firm, metal surface.*

BARK RINGING: *Removal of a narrow strip of bark from around all or part of the trunk of an apple or pear tree to encourage fruiting. Do not bark ring cherry, plum, gage, nectarine or peach trees.*

BLEEDING: *Loss of sap after a shoot or branch has been cut.*

BLIND: *Lacking a central growing tip.*

BOLE: *Trunk of a tree.*

BONSAI: *The art of growing, training and pruning shrubs, trees and conifers to remain small. Originally performed on outdoor plants, but recently tropical and subtropical plants have been trained as bonsai plants indoors.*

BOW SAW: *Large saw with a strong, metal frame. Ideal for cutting thick branches. It cuts on push strokes.*

BYPASS SECATEUR: *A type of secateur where one blade crosses the other.*

CALLUS: *Protective tissue formed by woody plants over wounds such as saw cuts.*

CHAIN-SAW: *Powered by electricity or a small internal combustion engine. Observe all safety rules when using one – they can be lethal!*

CANE FRUITS: *Create long, cane-like stems from ground level, which influences the way they are pruned.*

CLIMBING ROSES: *Have a more permanent framework of shoots than ramblers and produce shoots that develop flowers during the same year. This influences the way they are pruned.*

CLUSTER-FLOWERED ROSES: *Earlier known as floribunda roses. For pruning purposes, they are collectively known as bush roses.*

CORDON TREES: *Specially-trained fruit trees that grow at an angle of between 35 and 45 degrees on tiered wires. Often grown against a wall.*

DEAD HEADING: *Removal of dead flowers to prevent seed development.*

DECIDUOUS: *Tree or shrub that sheds its leaves in autumn and develops fresh ones in spring.*

DISBUDDING: *Removal of small flower buds from around a main one to encourage a larger flower.*

DORMANT: *Refers to the resting period, usually autumn and winter, when a plant makes little or no growth. Many plants – such as apples and pears – are pruned during this period.*

ELECTRICAL HEDGE TRIMMER: *Powered either by mains electricity or a rechargeable battery fitted into the appliance.*

ESPALIER: *Fruit tree trained so that its branches form tiers.*

EVERGREEN: *Shrub or tree that is continuously clothed in leaves. However leaves regularly die, while others develop, creating a green canopy.*

FAN: *Fruit tree trained so that its branches create the shape of a fan.*

FEATHERED: *Having branches all the way down the trunk of a tree.*

FLORIBUNDA ROSES: *Now officially known as cluster-flowered roses. For pruning purposes, they are known as bush roses.*

FORMAL HEDGES: *Types that are clipped to a clinical outline.*

FUNGICIDAL PAINT: *Used to cover large wounds in trees to prevent the entry of diseases.*

GRECIAN SAW: *A type of pruning saw with a curved, narrow blade that cuts on a pull stroke.*

HAND PRUNERS: *A North American term used to describe secateurs.*

HARD PRUNING: *Usually used to refer to the way bush roses are pruned.*

HEDGING SHEARS: *Used to trim hedges as well as ericaceous plants. Some shears have a notch at the bases of the blades to enable thick stems to be cut.*

HIGH PRUNING: *Another term for hard pruning when referring to bush roses.*

HIGH-REACH PRUNER: *Enables branches up to 3.6m/12ft high to be cut safely from ground level.*

HYBRID TEA ROSES: *Now known as large-flowered roses. For pruning purposes, they are collectively known as bush roses.*

KNOT GARDENS: *Type of garden formed of intricate designs, usually with clipped hedging plants.*

LARGE-FLOWERED ROSES: *Earlier known as hybrid tea roses. For pruning purposes, they are collectively known as bush roses.*

LATERAL SHOOT: *A shoot that arises from a stem or main shoot.*

LEADING SHOOT: *The top of the main stem.*

LEG: *A plant, such as a gooseberry, that has a short stem at its base.*

LEVER-ACTION LOPPERS: *Loppers with a special lever action enabling thick shoots to be severed.*

LIGHT PRUNING: *Usually used to refer to the way bush roses are pruned.*

LONG PRUNING: *Another term for hard pruning bush roses.*

LOPPERS: *Long-handled secateurs, used to cut thick shoots. Have either a bypass or anvil cutting action.*

LOW PRUNING: *Another term for light pruning when referring to bush roses.*

MAIDEN: *One-year-old fruit tree.*

MEDIUM PRUNING: *Another term for moderate pruning when referring to bush roses.*

MODERATE PRUNING: *Usually used to refer to the way bush roses are pruned.*

PARROT SECATEURS: *An earlier name for bypass secateurs, where one blade crosses the other.*

PARTIAL EVERGREEN: *Some shrubs, such as Privet* (Ligustrum ovalifolium) *remain evergreen in most climates, but in cold winters may lose their leaves.*

PLEACHING: *Creating hedges that appear to be on stilts. Lower branches are cut off and the upper ones trained to form a continuous screen of stems and leaves*

POLLARDING: *Cutting back all branches to the trunk. Usually, this drastic pruning has to be repeated within a few years. It results from planting trees in the wrong positions.*

POWER-BREAKER: *A device that instantly cuts off power to electrical equipment – essential when using electrical hedge trimmers or chain-saws.*

PRUNING: *The controlled cutting out of parts of plants to encourage the development of better flowers, regular fruit production and a long, healthy life.*

RAMBLING ROSES: *Create long, pliable shoots one year that develop flowers the following one. This influences their pruning.*

ROOT-PRUNING: *Involves digging a trench around part – or whole – of a tree to encourage fruiting.*

SECATEURS: *Used for pruning and known in North America as hand pruners. There are two types: anvil and bypass (earlier known as parrot secateurs). Both should be sharp and clean.*

SIDESHOOT: *A shoot that arises from a larger one.*

SPUR BEARING: *Some apples and pears produce fruits on short spurs.*

STOOL: *Plants – such as blackcurrants – that produce masses of shoots from ground level. Many dogwoods* (Cornus) *are grown in this way to encourage the production of fresh, young shoots.*

SUCKERS: *Shoots that develop from the roots of plants. Suckers can also arise on the stems of standard roses.*

SUMMER PRUNING: *Performed in summer and used to encourage the development of fruiting shoots and spurs without the risk of producing excessive growth. Usually performed on cordon, espalier and fan-trained trees.*

TIP BEARING: *Some apples and pears produce fruits towards the tips of branches. This influences the way they are pruned.*

TOPIARY: *The art of training and clipping evergreen shrubs to form shapes.*

WATER-SHOOTS: *Thin, pliable shoots that appear on trunks and main branches of some trees.*

INDEX